Reveal the Secrets of the SACRED ROSE

Reveal the Secrets of the SACRED ROSE

Steven Culbert

W. Foulsham & Co. Ltd.

London · New York · Toronto · Cape Town · Sydney

W. Foulsham & Company Limited
Yeovil Road, Slough, Berkshire, SL1 4JH

ISBN 0–572–01502–X

Printed in Great Britain at
St Edmundsbury Press, Bury St Edmunds

CONTENTS

The Tarot Path to Wisdom

Now view these cards in wonder
Their mystique here preserved
Your past, your present and future
Given here without reserve.

To waken all your knowledge
Your psyche thus inspired
You need no longer be a *HERMIT*
Or wait on your *LOVERS'* word.

Your *WHEEL* can turn full cycle
Until your *JUDGEMENT* day
Where with *STRENGTH'S* help the *CHARIOT*
Will chase your *DEVILS* away.

And if upon *DEATH'S* doorstep
Your *HIGH PRIESTESS* you call,
With *LIGHTNING* speed *MAGICIANS*
Will judge a poor *FOOL'S* worth.

Then *JUSTICE'S* great wisdom
Will a *HANGED MAN* bring to rest
And the *MOON'S* own self-delusion
Will in a *POPE'S* arms be blessed.

Now the *EMPEROR* is settled,
With *TEMPERANCE* and grace,
A *WORLD* reborn with an *EMPRESS*
That *STAR* struck dreamers make.

Set your *SUN* ablaze with energy
To ensure a bright new day,
For the tarot cards as you will learn
Will always lead the way.

THE TAROT REVEALED

The tarot cards are a collection of symbols presented through an ancient pack of 78 cards which have no proven historical beginning. For centuries they have been surrounded with a mystique which many believed only the initiated or blessed were able or meant to interpret, yet this is not the truth at all. Who originally created these cards cannot be discovered by even our most gifted historians and their origins are disputed in many schools of thought. Be they a gift from the gods, or a creation of man matters not, as long as their true value to us all is appreciated. For too long they have been misused and misrepresented by the few that have attempted to solve their mysterious origins, who played on the superstitions of those less informed. I hope here to assist in the changing of this situation.

Everyone who breathes upon this earth is a part of the symbolism within the tarot and everyone who learns to look at the cards with the correct perspective could become the so-called expert. All you need is the patience and application of any child studying maths or English at school. The human psychic or sixth sense is alive in us all, was given freely at birth and awaits only our application of its energies to be of use to us. The symbolic pictures and meanings of the cards, which seem to awaken that latent ability within us is not open for discussion within the pages of this manuscript. You would not be reading these pages if you were not at least curious about its existence, but what I hope to achieve that so many before have failed is the right perspective with which you view and thereafter utilise that psychic ability. For this reason, the Sacred Rose tarot has been chosen from the minefield of different packs available today.

What is different about this pack? To this I answer with the following three points. Firstly, they are fully symbolically illustrated. In other words the messages in the cards are in picture form. Secondly, they are 'colourgenisised'. That is to say that the arrangement of colours within the cards is within the scope of modern colour psychology. Thirdly, they are easily available through specialist high street bookshops or suppliers.

So with these three points in mind, we have already reduced our problems by finding a readily available product, properly illustrated and coloured with faces and figures which relate to today's world, rather than to our medieval past. Tarot cards should properly be described as a book of symbolic pictures which deal with all the events and eventualities that could occur in one's life. They awaken within you knowledge about yourself or those around you that perhaps before went unnoticed, yet when laid before you in a pattern selected at random form a picture of those circumstances that you can then recognise. The pictures attune you to your own subconscious reasoning or intuition. Inspired as you now may be to read on, remember that a study of the tarot in this manner is designed to alter the way it has been perceived in the past by experienced students of the tarot, or to set a correct perspective for those just beginning to find an interest. The human psychic sense is based upon the imaginative abilities possessed by us all. It develops in response to our social behaviour patterns, in response to the toys we played with and the environments in which we were raised. A study of the book of tarot as a pack of cards used for divination relies heavily upon this imaginative energy which is perhaps why so many give different interpretations of the same energies within the individual cards, each individual firmly convinced that they are correct in their own interpretation. Each is correct in their own way. What they have failed to achieve that we attempt now is the ability to awaken your own individual imaginative psychic energy and apply this to the energy of the symbolism of different cards in relation to your own circumstances. The meanings for the cards in this manuscript are therefore my own imaginative interpretation, conditioned by my own social upbringing. Your background and experience will be different. The point, however is that you should follow the same methods of application.

I hope that by showing you how I arrived at my own conclusions you may reach your own and awaken the insight given to you at birth which can thereafter be utilised in many areas of your life and not just in interpreting the tarot cards.

TAROT
CARDS

Buying your first pack of tarot cards is like buying a
chess board having never read the rules or seen how the
pieces move around the board. Yet the more you play the
game the quicker you comprehend its rules and moves
and the relationships between pieces when they oppose or
move in unison with others. Your new pack of tarot cards
should be treated in a similar manner. The more you
handle, view and meditate upon the symbolism within
the different cards, the quicker they will be retained in
your memory. We will not deal here with the spiritual
growth which many believe then follows, rather we leave
that to the many authors who have dealt with it in its
own right. It is my belief however that knowledge brings
maturity and understanding as a natural process and the
more you handle and familiarise yourself with your cards,
the sooner you may attain that maturity. The belief that
many have that allowing others to handle your cards will
affect your ability to read them is in my opinion
psychological. Your car does not refuse to start because
your partner drives it. You are the interpreter of the
symbolism linked through your imaginative psyche. You
are the trigger, the battery and power source. The cards
are merely the tools which allow you to find the track
you were seeking. For too long now superstition and
misguidance have created an aura of inaccessibility
around tarot cards. You are the new aquarian generation
of communicators who will dispel these old myths and
bring into the light your truths. Let us look at some of

the superstitions and try to rationalise them. For example: 'Always keep your cards bound in silk and in a locked box when not in use or on your person'. A great idea but what practical use has it? It is a ritualistic practice designed to teach patience and respect for the cards and what they may do for you. A good idea perhaps, but do we live in an age where respect for knowledge must be ritualised and does the silk really prevent energy from leaving the cards affecting our ability to interpret their meanings? I was always of the opinion that the interpretation came from me and I for one do not see how wrapping myself in silk will reflect my ability as a tarot reader. Wrap your cards in silk by all means, but to keep them from being soiled or damaged not to improve your ability to interpret their symbolism. As for the box, I have never possessed one and my cards are usually on my desk top in my consultation room when not in my pocket on their way to a group sitting or house party.

Another superstition is never to allow others to handle your cards out of curiosity. I encourage it. The more people who handle the cards and awaken their own desires to delve further into the secrets they hold the better. Yet again this superstition dwells on the fear that those who handle your cards taint them, but it is you who interpret the symbolism of the cards, not they that use you. The only exception to this rule would be for those who practise 'psychometry' with their cards. Psychometry is the sensed link made when handling objects into which others have put emotional energy. But this is not interpreting the symbolism of the tarot and therefore does not apply to what we have set out to achieve in this book. One last superstition which many foster is that your cards must be a gift from another and not purchased by you. I can only state that for some 15 years I have purchased my own tarot cards and they have always served me well. The only pack I ever received as a gift from another person was not to my taste is the design of the cards and I never used them professionally. The superstition was begun by those too mean to buy their own in order that others would make the purchase for them!

By all means develop your imagination when trying to perceive the messages within the symbolism of the tarot cards, but don't allow superstition to hamper or give you excuses for not recognising the true source of its messages – that of *your* psychic imagination finding an outlet through the symbolism within the cards. I have been a tarot reader for almost 15 years, have taught many students who scoffed at the paranormal and were unable to perceive a hidden part of their minds they had blinded themselves to. No-one doubts the psychologist with his ink blots which you interpret through your imagination and from which he or she then makes a diagnosis and yet the psychologist is behaving like a tarot reader. Based on your imaginative response to certain ink blots, the psychologist applies a mental attitude to the class and environment that you were brought up in and in which you live. He then offers advice on how he may cure or help your situation. The tarot reader should use the same ingredients of imagination and symbolic effects upon the client and their circumstances. The only difference being that the tarot reader accepts the power of the psychic imagination and makes good use of it.

THE SACRED ROSE TAROT

It would be an omission to write a book on the Sacred Rose tarot without giving the reader some background to its history and the reasons for selecting it as one of the more special packs available today. Not all the views within this book will agree with those of the creator of this pack in the divinatory sense.

The Sacred Rose tarot first came into being when Stuart R. Kaplan was attracted to a piece of artwork which arrived on his office desk one day in 1977. Though the artwork was not directly relevant to tarot cards, it inspired Mr Kaplan to contact the artist with a view to seeing other works. The artist was Johanna Sherman. A meeting between the two was arranged and Mr Kaplan commissioned Mrs Sherman to paint the first 'major arcana' card, the Fool. The results obtained must have pleased Mr Kaplan because he then commissioned Mrs Sherman to complete the remaining 21 cards. Over the next six months, the artist prepared many sketches of the cards which Mr Kaplan and Mr Bennet the art director of US Games Inc discussed and finally, in July 1978, Mrs Sherman agreed to complete the 78 card pack in two stages. The 22 major arcana were followed by the 56 minor arcana. When the major arcana was completed in 1980 the original drawing of the Fool, which was the card that had inspired Mrs Sherman to draw this tarot pack and Mr Kaplan to commission it, was modified so that it matched the style of the remaining cards. This then gave us the Sacred Rose tarot of today. The design on the back of the Sacred Rose tarot cards was inspired by the sacred lotus of the Orient depicting five roses entwined in a lattice of branches and resting on a bed of green leaves. This symbol of the rose represents the fertility of nature and is included throughout the tarot pack on different cards as a clue to the outcome of the energies of the cards. The interpretations are:

> Red Rose for Sacrifice
> White Rose for Purity
> Blue Rose for Impossibility.
> Gold Rose for Absolute Achievement
> Purple Rose for Time and Space.

This is one of the features which makes this pack special amongst so many others. The Roses can be interpreted also as:

> Red Rose for *energy wisely used or wasted*
> White Rose for *ideas and creative enterprises*
> Blue Rose for *emotional energies used or abused*
> Gold Rose for *possessions and worldly affairs*
> Purple Rose signifies *spiritual matters*.

They could also be linked to the elements of creation, Earth, Air, Fire and Water combining to create Ether.

THE MAJOR ARCANA

We shall deal with the major arcana in the first instance and each of the following pages will give a description of each card and the basic meaning of the symbols it contains, as well as a guide to how the colouring of the pictures creates an energy for each symbol. A simple divinatory expression will also be included for the symbols as an indicator for their meaning. Remember that you should also follow your own psychic imagination and create your own explanations for the symbolism if you are to become a competent tarot card reader. Remember our divinatory expressions are a guide based on all the symbolism within a card. However, on most occasions when divining with the tarot you will be drawn to one particular aspect of the card like contemplating a chess board, but only really seeing the situation that affects your king. Your knights and pawns may be important pieces later but you must solve the king's position for them to be of any future use. This is the situation where you must apply your psychic imagination to the existing circumstances. On the chess board the threat may be a queen, rook or one of a thousand combinations of the pieces. With the knowledge of how the chess pieces move you can plan your escape or attack, or see your future plights or potential. The tarot cards work in a similar fashion.

Each card has specific energies and is capable of suggesting different moves, depending on the pressures it is under. You must decide what those pressures are and where the next move will take you from the energies which your psychic imagination perceives. The rest is simplicity itself – a series of logical applications of perceived energies, which give you the outcome, or answers, which were always in your subconscious but which you had failed to see until the cards revealed them to you.

In chess, the king is always strong with his castles on his flanks and the queen by his side, just as certain tarot card energies are stronger when linked to some cards and weaker when aligned with others. If you are to become the chess master of the tarot, you must learn the moves that each card is capable of making, apply the strength of the move it can make to the existing circumstances and then you need never hear the words 'check mate' again.

0
THE
FOOL

The Fool has an unusual position amongst the major arcana being both the card which can come at the beginning or the end. In some packs it has the number 0 while in others 22.

The card depicts the figure of a young boy or man dressed in a red shirt, symbolising his enthusiastic nature. He wears purple mountain trousers to the knee, the colour indicating his spiritual knowledge, the style his immaturity. On his head sits a cap with a red and a purple bobble, these colours indicating the balance he must seek through personal endeavour between the physical and spiritual aspects of himself. His green belt suggests productivity and security through the balance of the scales of justice. His white leggings with crossbanded red leather suggest the trails he must take or ladder he must climb to attain purity of self. Across his right shoulder he carries a bag of worldly possessions and the purple here indicates karmic responsibilities.

In his right hand he holds a white rose showing that his aims may be pure, but perhaps irrational for a white dog pulls at his left leg as if in warning about the unknown cosmic influences he is about to encounter. Above his head flutters a brightly coloured butterfly, a creature which undergoes great changes from caterpillar to chrysalis only to be reborn with the power of flight. This image suggests that the Fool will, by the lessons he learns, develop from the '0' beginner to the '22' adept, or teacher. In the background is the kabbalistic Tree of Life through which the Fool has passed. He now has the

knowledge, but must step forth into the cosmos to find
fertile soil upon which to build his dreams. All around
him flowers burst forth in new growth and bloom in
varied colours. They grow from infertile rocks and
crevices and this is the final clue to the path of the Fool.
If the task is worthy, then no matter what the opposition
or terrain, success and a harvest can be achieved with
perseverance.

Divinatory Meaning

Positive: Innocence. A spiritual awakening. Visions of
youth being realised by the old. A karmic lesson or
responsibility. A task which others see as foolhardy, but a
necessity to the one about to undertake it.

Negative: A fool who thinks not of the consequences of
their actions, being blind to its effects. One with a loose
and foolish attitude or tongue. A fool and his possessions
are soon parted. A gullible individual who believes too
easily and without question. Apathy, foolish action and
insanity.

1

THE
MAGICIAN

The card depicts a young man who appears to float
unsupported as if by some feat of magic, while around
him is an aura of light. His face is serene, even
complacent about those lesser mortals around him, for he
believes in the power of his magical abilities to take him
beyond the problems of his fellow man. The reddish
purple robe he is wearing indicates he has spiritual

energy, but may be tempted to misuse it through rash or hasty actions and though he may appear serene he can be quick to react to movements around his domain. The double nimbus above his head symbolises masculinity and femininity, esoteric knowledge and the ability to blend together the essences of the heavens and worldly life, while the talisman bag around his neck indicates that his faith in himself is not as strong as he would have us believe, else why should he require its protection? Around him are the symbols of the four suits, or elements, depicting his mastery of the elements and the ability to summon them to his aid should he need to do so. Either side of him multi-coloured roses spring to life where he treads, as if his passing brought them to life. The baton in his left hand indicates that knowledge must be grasped if it is to be of any use. Knowledge becomes of practical value through the transmission of its energy to the pentacle below his right hand. The trees in the background are his pillars to give him support and protect him from behind.

Divinatory Meaning

Positive: Creativity and intelligence. The ability to see what others have failed to notice and make practical use of that knowledge for personal ends. The beginnings of spiritual evolution and self-recognition.

Negative: Trickery. The misuse of knowledge for self-gain at the expense of others. Selfishness and self-indulgence. Risks which are unnecessary and satisfy only one's own ego and vanity.

2
THE HIGH PRIESTESS

The card depicts the High Priestess sitting upon her wordly throne. She appears as though majestic and chaste and represents the virgin aspects of magical and spiritual energy. Those who gaze upon her experience a feeling of awe. Her dark, bushy flowing hair suggests things which are hidden and guarded by her mysterious nature, while the crown of Mercury on her head suggests the ability to communicate the unknown and a deep knowledge of the hidden arts. The astral veil between the two pillars of the Tree of Life, which appears to hide the background from view, acts as a bridge between the two forces of Boaz (B) being the dark nature of Water and Earth and Jachin (J) the elemental forces of Fire and Air. The High Priestess becomes the pivot, or balance, between these forces allowing them an interaction that without her presence would be without control. The golden triangle above her head held aloft by the green leaves of the Tree of Life indicates wisdom and creativity, through Kether (godhead), Binah (intelligence) and Chokmah (wisdom) thus forming the triad. She is dressed in a blue robe and the outer crown on her head is of the same colour indicating emotional attunement and understanding. Across her breast is a solar cross linking the heavens to the earth while she points at the book of knowledge indicating that she has the abilities to teach those who would pay her heed. The gown beneath the book becomes almost purple, as a sign that the spirituality of the lesson is perhaps most important. Her feet rest upon a crescent Moon, the symbol of the divine nature of her spirituality while roses bloom all around her, emphasising that knowledge brings birth, power and renewal.

Divinatory Meaning

Positive: Change in circumstances through understanding and removal of emotional obstacles before the next new moon.

Negative: Emotional energies block progress. Detachment is necessary from decisions to be made.

Note. The High Priestess always has a special effect in any tarot spread and will always bring enlightenment, even if we learn by our mistakes.

3
THE EMPRESS

The card depicts a motherly figure, who appears to be pregnant and therefore represents fertility. She sits on her throne symbolising her authority, yet despite her power and authority she is available to all who would seek her out. The twelve stars above her head symbolise the twelve signs of the zodiac. She is the queen of the universe. In her left hand she holds a sceptre topped with the orb of Mercury and the solar cross similar to those worn by the High Priestess. Worldly power is hers for the taking, yet connected to the long stem of the sceptre these symbols also link to the male as catalyst of the female's fertility. She is dressed in a blue robe, indicating her emotional depths and wears the gold rose at her breast symbolising creative achievements. The necklace of seven pearls visible around her neck indicates her power over the seven chakras of the Hindus. The shield before her legs bears the symbol of Venus with the purple and green background indicating feminine intuition and spirituality. Her feet rest upon the crescent Moon as an indication of her emotional control and infinite understanding. She sits upon a red cushion, an indicator of the hidden reserves of energy she can draw upon when helping others. The overall yellow–gold background indicates that her knowledge is infinite, while her throne is moulded from the natural world and is unshakeable.

The roses are in full bloom all around her feet, another sign of her abundance. This card shows that the High Priestess has at last found her soul mate and can now surrender her virginity and become the childbearing Empress who will eventually give birth to a divine child (idea) with the Emperor.

Divinatory Meaning

Positive: Natural instincts and intuition should be followed and success will be attained. Often appears at the time of a birth in the family, or new business venture.

Negative: Unbalanced and vain opinions will result in wasted energies and empty achievements. Can indicate aborted or lost children.

4
THE EMPEROR

This card indicates the bearded figure of a powerful yet spiritual man upon a throne wearing a purple robe. The red background indicates Fire and strength while above his head is an eagle, the symbol of wisdom, showing that his energies are directed with reason. The eagle is also an indicator of the hunter and while the Emperor at present sits upon his throne, he can at will take flight and start his hunt. Upon his head is a crown with seven points or chakras indicating that he is spiritually aware and developed and that his spirituality is expressed through his intelligence. In his right hand he holds a sceptre topped with a fleur-de-lis, showing his connections with nature. The thick, long staff reiterates his masculinity and physical power. The golden orb in his left hand shows his need for feminine intuition and partnership as well as the value he places upon his partner, the Empress. On his feet are heavy boots which protect him from the elements. He sits on a golden throne indicating that his base of power is creativity, the protection of the elements and the ability to make solid the projects he begins.

This card is the masculine counterpart of the Empress, the seed which brings forth her fertility or the physical energy which can turn ideas into reality.

Divinatory Meaning

Positive: Wisdom through trial and error. Creativity and lessons well learned. Self-discipline and action to

bring about realisation. Authority, protection and
self-control.

Negative: Lack of self-control, emotional outburst
leading to physical anger and ruin. Over-confidence,
self-delusion and the annoyance of those in authority.

5

THE
HIEROPHANT

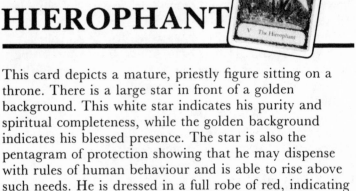

This card depicts a mature, priestly figure sitting on a
throne. There is a large star in front of a golden
background. This white star indicates his purity and
spiritual completeness, while the golden background
indicates his blessed presence. The star is also the
pentagram of protection showing that he may dispense
with rules of human behaviour and is able to rise above
such needs. He is dressed in a full robe of red, indicating
the energy which both protects him and which he has at
his command as an inner strength. On his head rests the

triple crown which indicates that his energy comes from the heavens to the earth. In his left hand he holds a sceptre topped with a triple cross with seven bars indicating his knowledge of the seven deadly sins (pride, envy, sloth, wrath, lust, gluttony and avarice) and the seven virtues (power, grace, ethics, courage, love, benevolence and honesty). Through the power of his staff, the Hierophant hopes he may fight evil and bring forth the good in all men. The golden cross upon his chest is an indicator of the manifestation of the spirit here on earth and while similar to that of the High Priestess, the vertical bar is stronger. His right hand is raised as if blessing those who have selected him, yet the glove on his hand leaves one contemplating the source of his blessing and the power behind it. Spiritual growth brings about changes and it is the Hierophant who sanctions and blesses, or condemns, those changes, be they for better or worse.

Divinatory Meaning

Positive: Alliances and partnerships, spiritual and social betterment and knowledge. The good advice of a friend or associate. A time to expand beyond oneself.

Negative: Rules have been broken because of weak morals, bad advice, prejudice and snobbery. The reappraisal of a decision is necessary.

6
THE
LOVERS

The card depicts the blindfolded figure of the angel
Raphael with a rising sun behind him. This indicates the
new dawn and the coming of spring and a time for
growth. His blindfold is blue showing that dreams can
come true. Beneath the angel sits a young man, Adam,
who embraces two female figures, Eve and Lilith, who
symbolise good and evil. Adam is solar and the seed of
growth and he must choose between the two aspects of
the lunar nature, the light and good of Eve, or the dark
nature of Lilith. Eve on his right side reaches out into the
cosmos, indicating her sense of purpose and desire for
womanhood, while Lilith on the left recoils against Adam
with a great strength of will leaving him to choose
between them. He and he alone, must make that choice,
or strive to be the balance between the two. The angel is
blindfolded and can be of no assistance to him. The
Lovers represents that part of us all which must decide
between the things we desire that would make us content
and the things which are rightly ours. Every man and
woman must make that choice for themselves. The
triangle which the three figures make symbolises the
eternal triangle.

Divinatory Meaning

Positive: The choice of which direction to take is now
yours. Your will is your own, do not allow others to
make decisions for you. Growth can be your reward if
you make the correct choice.

Negative: Choice is clouded by the opinions of others and you allow the desire for pleasure and ease to destroy that which you could have achieved in later life.

This card often appears in spreads when adultery may occur, or when more than one partner vies for attention, though it also indicates decisions to be made soon. Spring is always around the corner for those who select this card, though some must learn by their own mistakes.

7
THE CHARIOT

The card depicts a chariot drawn by two sphinxes, with tree roots for reins. There is the figure of a young man in the chariot. The sphinxes appear to be stepping into the cosmos, symbolising the ability to reach beyond one's limits. The dark sphinx on the right and the light sphinx on the left represent positive and negative forces. The sphinx in Greek mythology was a winged creature formed by the body of a lion with the head of a woman and which killed all who could not answer its riddle, "What walks on four legs in the morning, two in the afternoon and three in the evening?" The answer is the human, who crawls at birth, walks as an adult and with a walking stick in old age. The sphinx is a guardian of the knowledge not meant to be understood by mortals. This is indicated by the fact that it is the roots of the trees (nature) which form the reins while the charioteer fails to steer his own vehicle.

There are thirteen stars above the rider's head, five either side and three in his crown. In numerology, the number thirteen reduces to four, symbolising the foundations of knowledge which can be built upon.

Across the charioteer's shoulders are two moon plates which symbolise his ability to bring to reality the emotions and dreams of the subconscious. His clothing is purple and blue, indicating that the imagination and the spirit are closely linked. The red wheels of his chariot indicate Fire and the energy to overcome obstacles placed before him. Between the sphinxes is a red pentagram showing energy with a blue rose showing that he can overcome the impossible with the strength of his imagination. The reins of the sphinxes pass up the trunks of the tree through his moon shoulder pads revealing that forces beyond his comprehension guide him upon his path to achievement, though he may never understand fully the part they played. The rod in his right hand is topped with a pyramid mounted on a cube which is in turn positioned on a sphere of energy, indicating that a foundation of love and a sense of completion are accomplished through oneself alone. Only by fully utilising the energies you possess can you ever hope to achieve your true goals. This card is an indicator that only through self-mastery can one find one's true path and place in the scheme of things.

Divinatory Meaning

Positive: Victory can be achieved against even the most adverse conditions if the will and self-discipline are adhered to. There is no victory without effort or satisfaction without trial.

Negative: Misdirected will or singlemindedness will lead to empty victories or hollow achievements. You must direct your energies to that which you are capable of achieving.

8
JUSTICE

The card depicts the figure of a woman blindfolded and dressed in a red and purple robe. A triple crown rests on her head while in her right hand she holds a sword and in the left a set of scales with a blue rose in one half and a heart in the other. Her hair appears to growl like the lion's mane in a cosmic storm and on either side of her strong trees grow to form a canopy of green. Blue and red flowers bloom all around her. Her purple blindfold is a symbol of her ability to discriminate between good and evil and strengthens her intuition, while her red–purple robe indicates the essence of her spiritual and physical power and energy. The triple crown represents her creative ability while her flaming red hair emphasises the power she has to create from the energies at her disposal.

The sword in her right hand forms an inverted triangle and the blending of the essences of Fire and Water, confirming that inspired intellect leads to true justice. The three red stones in the hilt show she has the fire to accomplish the tasks she begins. The scales show a balance between the red heart of humanity and compassion, while on the other side the blue rose of impossibility is held in balance. Neither outweighs the other. Both hang in the balance, yet at any moment it could tip either way. Justice's main effect in a tarot card spread is to indicate how a balance between desire and its impossibility may be achieved with honour. She indicates where you may be tipping your scales (decisions) out of balance, or how you may maintain an equilibrium. The energies of this card set tests which must be passed before the responsibilities of future success can be realised.

Divinatory Meaning

Positive: The weighing of possibilities for decisions to be made. Tests and ordeals which can be surmounted. Legal conflict or litigation which can be resolved.

Negative: Biased and one-sided opinions which can lead to bitterness, conflict and ruin. Rash actions, which later may be regretted.

9
THE
HERMIT

This card depicts the solitary figure of the Hermit in the form of an old man, bearded, cloaked and possessed of an unquenchable thirst for knowledge. The Hermit is the outsider, the one who seeks his own way to self-enlightenment and, while he possesses many priestly habits, he is not ordained, but is more the scholar than the priest, the teacher rather than the leader. He is dressed in a red robe. The colour would indicate sacrifice rather than the Fire energy of self-indulgence and he carries in his right hand a lantern whose exposed flame illuminates his way and reveals to him hidden secrets, thus increasing his knowledge. In his left hand he holds the crooked staff of green, the symbol of his understanding and control of the forces of nature which help him on his path. The staff also protects him against many dangers and is a symbol of his caring and understanding for his flock. Behind him stand two Trees of Life which indicate his passage from the physical world through the barrenness of self-sacrifice to the cosmic garden of the sacred roses, into which his right foot falls. This card's energies indicate that if one is to obtain spiritual growth one must experience self-denial and tread an individual path. The rewards of this in both knowledge and understanding are well worth the journey.

Divinatory Meaning

Positive: Knowledge of the inner self holds the key to problems. Spiritual growth brings its own rewards and understanding. The search for truth.

Negative: False humility and self-deception bring about loneliness and self-delusion. A fear of the truth, failure to face the reality of current circumstances.

10
THE WHEEL
OF FORTUNE

The card depicts a wheel of purple with flashes of blue-green and pink. The purple wheel symbolises the power of the gods, the green suggests its links with nature, the blue with man's desires or dreams and the pink with the compassion of rewards which can be obtained. On the right of wheel is the god Anubis, the positive force of nature whose left hand appears to be trying to control the motion of the wheel, while the winged serpent is Typhon, the evil god of self-destruction and hidden knowledge who would destroy you with your own greed. Within the wheel by Typhon rests an eagle symbolising intellect and the ability to win through, while next to Anubis swings a monkey who is dexterous and mischievous by nature and may be able to out-manoeuvre the gods. The wheel itself represents the divine intervention of the gods over which we as mortals have no control.

The backdrop of the card shows that all are watched over by the sphinx, who knows and understands the forces at play before her and waits patiently for her moment to act. The principle meaning of the card is to indicate that without trial and perseverance accomplishment is worthless. If you are to seek the treasures of the gods you must play them at their own game with the skill of the monkey and the intellect and courage of the eagle if you truly desire to pull off the impossible. Interaction on this level however is karmic and though you may feel you are your own master or mistress, you are a tool of the gods with a lesson to learn.

The rewards will show how you stood up to their tests.

Divinatory Meaning

Positive: Destiny, good fortune if you should pass the trials set out for you. Good conduct always brings its own rewards.

Negative: Self-delusion is no refuge from lessons you must learn. The severity of the lesson is increased by not grasping its meaning sooner.

11
STRENGTH

The card depicts the figure of a woman powerful enough to ride upon the back of a docile lion. In the background stand the Trees of Life. In this card the sense of distance is an indicator of the lengths one must sometimes go to in order to obtain success, or the realisation of one's ambitions. The woman symbolises the intuitive and spiritual energies of her sex, while the lion symbolises masculine strength. It is only by both working together as a team and in union that real success is achieved. The indicator is also a pointer to the fact that we are all a combination of masculinity and femininity and that we must achieve a balance between the two, rather than live the energies of one only. Physical and spiritual, animal and intellect. The female's hair is swept back as by a wind indicating the unification of their energies, while the double nimbus above her head indicates that this unification is divine and blessed in nature. The garden in full bloom around them indicates the birth and renewal which this unified energy can produce and as they are poised upon the edge of the cosmos nothing is beyond the capabilities of this divine energy.

Strength indicates the struggle in mankind between the animal and spiritual life, masculinity and femininity, positive and negative. Its lesson is that each by itself is incomplete, yet harnessed together their nature is divine and unstoppable.

Divinatory Meaning

Positive: Nothing is worthy of capture without effort. Sacrifice is never as severe as it is feared and with willpower and strength victory will be attained. A test of the soul's balance between the spiritual and physical self.

Negative: Failure of a spiritual test. Too much physical force is used to accomplish needs. Self-delusion brings self-destruction, bad temper and illness.

12
THE HANGED MAN

The card depicts the figure of a man hanging upside down from a vine on the Tree of Life. His face is at peace and although he is upside down he shows no fear of his predicament. His hands are clasped as if in prayer and his left leg crosses behind his right and appears to point towards the Tree of Life in the background as if his knowledge keeps him free from fear. His trousers are red indicating his physical self while his shirt is purple symbolising his spiritual knowledge. His hands clasp a red rose symbolising that physical sacrifices have brought him spiritual rewards and awareness, while the green vine which holds him aloft to the Tree of Life shows that the tree and its knowledge are his moral and spiritual support.

All around him flowers bloom symbolising his new awakening and the flowering of his efforts. The Hanged Man symbolises the transformation between the emotional and physical needs and the interaction that takes place between them. It is indicative of the effect of emotional desires upon the physical self and how balance may be achieved.

Divinatory Meaning

Positive: Faith in oneself through trial and error. Old ideals and beliefs put to the test. Self-sacrifice brings its own rewards. Emotional fulfilment through physical sacrifice. A period of waiting.

Negative: Selfish, emotional desires bring ruination. Lack of self-esteem and insecurity cloud the ability to make accurate assessments of situations. Defeat through selfishness and indecision.

13
DEATH

The card depicts the figure of Death as a hooded skeleton with a scythe. It is the only figure on the card and this is one of only a few cards which depict a figure rising from the cosmos and therefore representing divine intervention on earth. On this card, the figure's right foot is in contact with the physical earth and beneath his foot flowers have died, symbolising his ability to regenerate and change. Before each new spring a winter must pass and before a rebirth sacrifices must be made. Around the figure of Death are some fertile places where flowers bloom indicating that physical death is not a complete death, but leads to regeneration.

The figure wears a purple robe indicating his spiritual rebirth and energy and he steps towards the solar side of the card indicating that the transformation of the physical body is not the end of the spiritual or astral existence. In his left hand he holds a scythe. The shape of the blade represents lunar emotions. The interplay of solar and lunar cycles indicates the passing of time, evolution and the need to move on and accept change.

Death is one of several cards within the tarot pack which indicate fatalistic circumstances beyond the control of the enquirer and the reader. They should be accepted and interpreted as cards of fate controlled by the gods. The other major arcana cards with this characteristic are: Justice, The Wheel of Fortune, The Hanged Man and The Tower. The effects represented by these cards are the result of divine intervention of a karmic nature in the life of the individual.

Divinatory Meaning

Positive: A time when the old must be laid to rest in order that the new may begin. Transitions and great changes which will change the life of the enquirer. A new cycle of events is to begin for the better.

Negative: Change is required and offered though it is not accepted. Failure to accept change creates a state of limbo. It is necessary to let go of the past and the effects it has had.

14
TEMPERANCE

The card depicts an angelic winged figure who pours a liquid between two vessels. The silver vessel represents the emotional self while the golden one represents the physical self. The liquid indicates the balance which must exist between the two containers before decisions are made. Temperance wears a red robe symbolising her passions and energetic emotions while the green lining symbolises her need to control and make practical use of them. Her feet are bare and in contact with both the earth and the cosmos, emphasising her ability to find the balance between physical and emotional or physical and spiritual being. She has golden wings indicating her solar energy and her belief in justice and intelligence. She is aware that the blending of the physical and emotional self creates a powerful energy which will bring her the victory she requires. The Trees of Life in this card are in the background indicating a metaphysical emergence or spiritual growth above and beyond the self. All around ferns and flowers of many colours and shapes bloom indicating the diversity and variety which can be born of the balance Temperance strives to attain.

Divinatory Meaning

Positive: With patience and thought the right moves are made at the right time and success is assured. The situation requires careful thought and consideration before action is taken. Observe, co-operate and moderate opinions to ensure success.

Negative: Forcing issues and allowing the emotions to influence judgement will lead to frustration. Poor management is no excuse for blaming others for errors.

15
THE
DEVIL

The card depicts the horned figure of the Devil seated upon a throne of dead trees. His crown of golden horns, lunar in shape, indicates his emotional being while the golden colour his solar self though his blending of these energies is purely physical or sexual. The pentagram upon his forehead is not inverted indicating that it is not beyond the card's comprehension to understand the illusion of power it has created for itself and that through intuition salvation and the right path may again be found.

The Devil's wings are purple indicating the spiritual power of the creatures of the night while the green body indicates the fertility of their evil intent. The red face indicates his vengeful, negative passions, while the goat-like legs indicate the strength and surefootedness with which his desires may creep up upon you. The flame between his horns burns with illusionary knowledge and the power of deception. His hands point upwards and downwards in the form of the kabbalistic blessing although in this case the distance between the two hands indicates his malevolent intentions. Beneath his feet are the figures of a man and woman possibly Adam and Eve. They are bound by the hands, but could easily cut their bonds. However, they remain in bondage tied by their own greed and desire for material gains. The Devil indicates bondage to an ideal situation or desire which could be broken by will power. The bondage is of the individual's own creation.

Divinatory Meaning

Positive: The attempting of that for which there has been no preparation. The breaking of bonds will bring order from chaos. Material indulgence, or the desire for carnal indulgence with others not of your ilk may cause harm.

Negative: You have the knowledge of what is right and wrong or good and evil and yet persist in the path of evil. You fool no-one but yourself and harm only those who truly care for you. You must rethink the stupidity of your desires and set yourself free from the limitations you have imposed upon yourself.

16
THE
TOWER

The card depicts the figures of a man and a woman dressed in purple robes falling from a tower which has been struck by lightning. The man and woman symbolise Adam and Eve, while the purple robes symbolise their spiritual fall. The tower which they had created is being destroyed by outside forces and they no longer control their own destinies because they chose to admire their own egos, symbolised by the crown at the top of the tower, rather than the true source of their creativity. The Tower card symbolises transformation and the test of an individual's creativity and intentions in life and warns those who allow false ideals to blind their true purpose of the consequences of their actions. The lightning bolt which has struck the tower represents those higher spiritual forces and their anger at self-righteousness and worship of the material rather than the spiritual. The tower has three windows which are symbolic of the two seeing eyes and the higher 'third eye', or psychic centre and warns us that all our actions are seen in the end and the consequences are then our own. The landscape around the tower is barren indicating that the promises of false gods offer no real reward and lead to desolation.

Divinatory Meaning

Positive: Old values are of no use now. Attention to circumstances must be made before it is too late to save anything. Unseen forces are at work beyond the control of the enquirer.

Negative: The clinging to old values and past ways means a failure to heed warnings bringing about downfall and destruction.

17
THE STAR

The card depicts a female figure who rests in the roots of the Tree of Life and is clothed in its foliage. Her unusual throne serves to give her the knowledge and strength to sit on the edge of the cosmos unafraid. With her right hand she waters the Tree of Life while with her left she pours her spiritual essences of intuition into the cosmos. The butterfly, depicted already on the card of the Fool, appears to rest upon her right hand symbolising metamorphosis and rebirth in the physical plane. Around her are three yellow stars symbolising her intellect and creativity coupled with philosophy while the four orange stars represent her pride and ambition. Her electrified hair of gold rises to show her genius in creativity against a background of the largest orange star which forms a pentagram of completeness. There are seven smaller stars which combine to symbolise the seven chakras, while the eighth red star or pentagram symbolises passion and desire. The eight stars together symbolise the eight paths to power through creativity, eight also being the number of regeneration.

The Star represents all things which require creative and intuitive direction, such as music, dance, meditation, love and psychic development. It is the card which grants the wishes of the imagination should you but create them on the physical plane of existence. All things which are worthwhile fall under the protection of this card and her blessing brings about their successful outcome.

Divinatory Meaning

Positive: The wish granted. Keep hope in your heart, your goals are attainable. Unexpected spiritual gifts will see that you come to no harm. An indicator of good health and benevolence.

Negative: Self-pity, fear and anxiety. Depression brought on by self-doubt and self-pity. Feelings of hopelessness are brought about by self-doubt. Stress and nervous disorders.

18
THE MOON
OF ILLUSION

The card depicts a female figure dressed in a green robe. She appears to dwell in the cosmos yet her robe clings to the tree in the background, indicating that she is suspended or in limbo between the two dimensions. Green is the colour of growth and fertility yet in this instance the clinging red crayfish indicates that her power is wasted because the fish must return to its own environment. She holds her left hand to her breast, while her right supports the moon indicating that she tries to exert too much control over her destiny while her purple hair is its real suport based in her esoteric and spiritual knowledge.

The moon sheds a tear undicating its own lack of control over the cycles of its rise and fall and its effect upon nature. Change is not always easy and often causes pain and anguish. Between the trees in the background a thin web suggests a link and entanglement which is emotionally based and self-initiated while the barren ground indicates that despair has taken over but should not have done so, for the figure has its feet planted in the cosmos and may draw upon its many energies, if so required. The Moon is the creator of self-delusion.

Divinatory Meaning

Positive: Old ways and values have been outgrown and must be cleared away if new growth is to occur. Self-pity and remorse should be set aside as hidden forces of great power can be brought into play for your favour should you see beyond the material.

Negative: Failure to let go of old values will blind you to the opportunities of the future. Self-delusion and self-praise are worth nothing. Rethink your strategy and stop deceiving yourself.

19

THE
SUN OF
ACCOMPLISHMENT

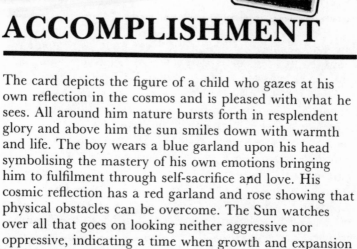

The card depicts the figure of a child who gazes at his own reflection in the cosmos and is pleased with what he sees. All around him nature bursts forth in resplendent glory and above him the sun smiles down with warmth and life. The boy wears a blue garland upon his head symbolising the mastery of his own emotions bringing him to fulfilment through self-sacrifice and love. His cosmic reflection has a red garland and rose showing that physical obstacles can be overcome. The Sun watches over all that goes on looking neither aggressive nor oppressive, indicating a time when growth and expansion can occur. The garden is a garden of delight and all the young boy need do is reach out and pluck the flower of his choice.

Divinatory Meaning

Positive: All obstacles can be surmounted and harmony achieved. The fulfilment of wishes with a period of happiness and joy.

Negative: The Sun is never negative, rather its energies are unused. Lonely people who lack friends means being out of attunement with nature, which is within your power to bring to fruition and into its correct balance.

20
JUDGEMENT

The card depicts the figure of a large angel with golden wings, suggesting solar power, whilst her yellow hair symbolises knowledge. The Tree of Life in the background has sustained the angel and given it the knowledge it requires to help mankind. With its solar power the angel is in a position to help mankind accomplish its resurrection. The two human figures represent Adam and Eve. Both are faced with a new beginning. Eve desired knowledge to be like God, while Adam's sin was to break the rules and disobey God's command. Each must now face the consequences of their actions and be reborn through the angel into their new existence, symbolised by the reborn child in front of the angel. The physical landscape is dead and barren yet the birth of the child suggests the benefits of the fruits of one's labours and the renewal of the resurrection.

Judgement represents each man's need to see himself as others do, to face up to the responsibility of his own actions and make good the mistakes of his past, for if he is not prepared to do so other forces will pass judgement.

Divinatory Meaning

Positive: The combination of the physical and spiritual self; opposites brought together bring about new beginnings and second chances. Divine help when required, the rewards for your past be they good or bad.

Negative: Inability to face up to actions of the past can cause delays or postponement of future projects. Lessons not learned and faced must be relearned in a harsh way.

21

THE WORLD

The card depicts a young woman dressed in a blue veil woven from the cloth of the gown of the High Priestess. She was once the Empress yet now with the birth of her child she is able to dance in happiness and joy. She balances upon her right leg to indicate her physical abilities, while in each hand she holds a baton symbolising the phallic sceptres of power that enable her to satisfy her needs. Encircling her is a laurel of roses indicating that she has gone full circle and attained completion. Victory is hers. Her golden hair emphasises her creativity which enabled her to come this far, while the intertwined branches of the Tree of Life behind her represent the harmony that the lessons have brought. A figure sits in each corner of the card. In the upper left, the man symbolises the element of Air, intellect and humanity, while in the upper right, the eagle symbolises the element Water, mental and emotional expression. To the lower left, the bull symbolises the element of Earth, the material plane of physical being, while to the lower right, the lion symbolises the element of Fire for strength, accomplishment and energy. The World has all elements at her disposal and combines them all to bring into being all the lessons she has learned.

The World symbolises that lessons have been well learned and knowledge of them retained. The owner of such knowledge can now step forth with confidence and experience growth on new levels.

Divinatory Meaning

Positive: Success and attainment through hard work and lessons well learned. The rewards of lessons are there for the taking. Completion.

Negative: Lessons poorly studied create uncertainty. Imperfection or poorly laid foundations will never stand the tests of time.

This completes our study of the major arcana, but before we move on to the minor let us first dwell upon that which is already stated. These are my explanations of the cards' symbolism as I see, feel and perceive them. Your perceptions need not be the same. Where I was first drawn to a blue veil about the figure of the World, you may be drawn to the eagle, bull or lion. The place that you are first drawn to is your starting point for interpretation of the energies depicted by a card. You must then be led by your psychic energy and intuition to develop the interpretation further.

THE MINOR ARCANA

The fifty-six remaining cards of the tarot deck are called the 'minor arcana' and are divided equally between four suits, with fourteen cards in each suit, similar to the structure of playing cards.

      The Swords are associated with the Spades

      The Batons, or Wands, with the Clubs

      The Cups, or Chalices, with the Hearts

      The Coins, or Pentacles, with the Diamonds.

Each suit has ten cards numbered X to 1 (ace) plus four court cards: King, Queen, Knight and Valet (or Page). It is the extra court card which adds the four extra cards to the tarot pack not seen in a pack of playing cards.

Each suit has a general effect upon areas of our lives and although I will be giving an interpretation for all the minor arcana in the following pages I shall first summarise the effects of each suit. Tarot cards are neither positive nor negative. They represent energies which we put to use. The way we apply these energies determines whether or not the effects are positive or negative.

Swords can be used to defend a kingdom or support a dictatorship. The application of the boldness and courage that the suit can endow upon the enquirer is a matter of choice.

While the major arcana represents spiritual evolvement and physical forces, the minor arcana relates to social status, occupations, etc. For example, the

Swords represent the characteristics of executives and the aristocracy, while the working class would have more in common with the Batons or Wands. The clergy and religious groups fall under the energies of the Cups or Chalices, while merchants, traders and retailers fall under the influence of Pentacles or Coins. Each suit has a direction in which its energies may be applied in relation to the questions of those who enquire. The significance and meaning of these energies will now be explained.

Suit of Swords

Swords represent force, strength and courage in the face of adversity. They symbolise that part of man which stimulates ambition, activity and progress, as well as accomplishment for good or bad. The cards' energies inspire qualities of leadership. They are the rulers of the element of Air and their expression through the mind gives them the power to dominate.

Suit of Batons

The Batons, or Wands, relate to the qualities of enterprise, particularly the enterprise of modest and humble people who strive to better their families and themselves. This is the suit of the worker or labourer and is epitomised by the clenched fist holding the budding baton or wand. Batons hold sway over the element of Fire.

Suit of Cups

Cups signify love, happiness, gaiety and joy, but are also the suit which deals with religion. Cups hold liquids and Water is the element which deals with passions, feelings and the compassionate nature of mankind.

Suit of Pentacles

Pentacle cards relate to the gain (or loss) of material possessions and to financial matters in general. Opportunists also come under their influence, although the merchant class has a sensitivity which is much misinterpreted by many. The element Earth hold sway over this group.

We are now left with the allocation of the court cards, which can be defined by type to elemental quality.

All Kings are of the mental expression of Air.
All Queens are of the emotional expression of Water.
All Knights are of the creative expression of Fire.
All Pages are of the material expression of Earth.

It is therefore now possible to link the different court cards, elementally, to find their expression thus:

The King of Swords is Air by suit and Air by card, while the King of Cups is Water by suit and Air by card.

The King of Cups has both Air and Water energies to draw upon, while the King of Swords has double air.

The following table indicates the elemental energies of the court cards.

Swords
King .... Air/Air
Queen .... Water/Air
Knight .... Fire/Air
Page .... Earth/Air

Cups
King .... Air/Water
Queen .... Water/Water
Knight .... Fire/Water
Page .... Earth/Water

Wands

King .... Air/Fire
Queen .... Water/Fire
Knight .... Fire/Fire
Page .... Earth/Fire

Pentacles

King .... Air/Earth
Queen .... Water/Earth
Knight .... Fire/Earth
Page .... Earth/Earth

One other point to note when you are interpreting your cards is that each of the suits can be associated with the astrological elements and to their associated astrological signs. This can help to date events, or place people under different rulerships. Thus:

> Batons relate to Leo, Aries and Sagittarius
> Swords relate to Gemini, Aquarius and Libra
> Cups relate to Pisces, Cancer and Scorpio
> Pentacles relate to Taurus, Capricorn and Virgo.

The court cards also give an indication of the ages of people you may encounter. Thus, Kings represent the mature man, while Queens represent the mature, or married woman. Knights represent the young man under 30, while Pages relate to the child, those about to enter puberty, virgins, or the innocent. Thus if the Knight of Pentacles appears in a romantic position, for a female client you would be able to signify that she was involved with or would come to know a young man with Fire and Earth ambitions, that is of an energetic yet practical nature, with a tendency to being possessive.

SUIT OF SWORDS

Ace of Swords

A hand grips the handle of a sword which emerges from a blue rose. The sword's blade is wrapped in thorns which stem from the rose.

Blue is the colour of emotional energy while swords reflect the intellect. The combining factor here is emotional knowledge which must be grasped, understood and acted upon before the situation becomes too harsh. The sword is held upright indicating action or battles to be fought, or that leadership is required to avoid distress. A new mental attitude or expression for feelings learned through personal sacrifice must be learned.

Divinatory Meaning

Positive: A realisation of the truth that was not perceived before. Knowledge which allows growth.

Negative: Anger and obsession blind mental judgement leading to depression and stubborness. You must change the way you handle your emotions if you are to achieve any recognition for your deeds.

Two of Swords

A man and a woman stand blindfolded facing each other, their swords stand at rest but are readily to hand. The moon shines above them but favours the passive feminine side indicating peace or a truce. The robes are purple and blue symbolising a spiritual emotional energy and although the couple are at present blindfolded, indicating a mental truce, the needs for change and greater harmony are still present, if the swords are to be laid to rest. This card indicates a partnership based upon mistrust or imbalanced mental attitudes which must be resolved if peace is to ensue.

Divinatory Meaning

Positive: A solution can be found and peace and harmony obtained, but both sides must present themselves with equality and equilibrium. Emotions and passions must be harnessed for the satisfaction of both partners and not sacrificed for the sake of one, if the peace is to continue.

Negative: Duplicity and falsehood reign. The falsehood shall be exposed and strife shall follow the treachery done. If you lie to others, you only lie to and fool yourself.

Three of Swords

A heart, in the centre of which is a blue rose, has been pierced by three swords. One sword strikes from above while two others from either side and below, causing the heart to bleed from the central sword. The heart is suspended between the barren branches of two trees. The three swords indicate intellectual endeavours, while the barren trees suggest that they have become redundant. The blue rose within the pink heart symbolises the arousal and expression of emotional passions. The pierced heart indicates an emotional loss which cannot be easily forgiven. This card indicates that matters have not progressed as planned and that some form of separation, isolation, strife or removal has occured which must be faced up to.

Divinatory Meaning

Positive: An emotional loss or a broken heart. Those you have trusted have failed to be worthy of your trust. Someone you are fond of is absent and you have not learned to accept this.

Negative: Mental stress as decisions of the past have proven to be miscalculations leading to anxiety, separation and a loss.

Four of Swords

A young knight sits under a moon in its first quarter. Behind him are four swords with their points driven into the ground and blood symbolising the battles of his past seeps into the ground. In his right hand he holds a blue rose symbolising the emotions he has spent, while at his left lies his helmet showing that he no longer needs to shield his thoughts. In front of him are two cups, one of which is shattered representing the emotional dreams he set out with, while the other is still whole symbolising his future ideals. His facial expression shows tranquility, as if after some ordeal. The foreground is barren indicating that plans for the future have yet to be made while the background is full of blooms indicating the fruits of his past. This card indicates that a period of rest is required before the next stage in the young man's life becomes active. It indicates rest and recuperation from the battles of his past.

Divinatory Meaning

Positive: A period of rest and recuperation is required before the next step is made. Contemplation of what is past will give the correct direction for the future.

Negative: The struggles of the past are still not fully dealt with and must be laid to rest if recuperation in preparation for the next phase is to occur. Arguments and quarrels can take place unexpectedly.

Five of Swords

A man is kneeling on the ground into which his blood seeps. He is impaled by four swords while a fifth hangs ready to deliver the final blow. Before him in his blood lies a blue rose while the moon above appears as if it is about to be eclipsed. Storm clouds brew and although he rests on fertile green land the landscape appears without hope.

The effect of this card is that of cruelty and malice either self-inflicted or wished upon someone by another. The cruelty is however mental rather than physical and is more indicative of one who is being mentally and emotionally drained or misused by another than representing any form of physical attack. Self-degradation or sacrifice that is unnecessary or unwanted, or self-crucifixion for a lost or useless cause may be indicated by this card.

Divinatory Meaning

Positive: The ill wishes that you think, or would like to inflict on others, harm you mentally far more than they ever would another and it is best that you put them out of your mind lest you punish yourself further.

Negative: The individual suffers from a weak will and preys on those even weaker in order to satisfy feelings of insecurity. Hollow victory is no victory and if this path is pursued desolation and isolation will ensue.

Six of Swords

A full moon is depicted in the background with a man and his family in what appears to be a boat on a cosmic ocean. His wife faces their future while he holds one sword upright in his left hand and the shepherd's staff of knowledge in the right. In the foreground, five swords are embedded in the ground, representing the man's past from which he attempts to escape or break free. This card indicates that changes in mental attitudes and states of consciousness bring about new hopes and realisations, while opening new avenues for expression. The boat indicates an emotional journey and although it is night the moon is full showing that there is knowledge or light enough to make the journey to bring about desired changes. Anxiety can be a thing of the past, if knowledge is utilised and projected into the future leaving behind that which would hamper progress.

Divinatory Meaning

Positive: A journey or voyage across water. A visit from those who have been away for some time. A good result from work done to overcome past disillusionment. Success at last, after anxiety, fear, or worry.

Negative: There is no immediate solution to the present difficulties as lessons of the past have remained unheeded. Stagnation comes as a result of foolish stubbornness to let go of that which is no longer needed.

Seven of Swords

The robed figure of a clown sits holding his dunce's cap. The upright swords representing courage are offered to him while two more point downwards indicating disapproval. Three swords rest before him and can be taken up should he choose to do so. The clown appears to lean forward either to grasp or reject what is before him, while the full moon above could light his way, should he decide to stir from his present position.

The seven of swords indicates the choices open to the individual who with insufficient planning knows not which way to turn. He fears his own courage, lacks the will to test his knowledge and seeks the easy way out, fearing to trust all. Thus, the card symbolises treachery, mistrust, the thief or the spy who watches all but never acts unless in his own interest.

Divinatory Meaning

Positive: Hopes and fantasy must be put aside and effort made to move forward, despite the uncertainty of the unknown. Confidences can be built upon but the seeker must make the first move.

Negative: Slander by those who are feared or trusted. The rejection of help based upon petty fears and quarrels. Treachery. Spies, who plot the downfall of others. Introverted loners, who fail to mix well with society.

Eight of Swords

The figure of a woman stands with one sword in her left hand while her right hand rests upon another. Six more swords pierce her gown as if holding her there. Her long black hair, symbolising her blindness, is blown in front of her while the full moon is reflected upon her robe in the foreground.

This card indicates blindness and self-limitation. The double moon represents conflicting emotions which leave her with the inability to see beyond the situation at hand. Her emotions have blinded her thought processes. The card is coloured only in the blue cosmos and the purple robe, symbolising spiritual stagnation brought upon by emotional blindness. This card indicates mental exhaustion brought about by excessive emotional energy which could lead, if unchecked, to mental breakdown. The limitations are self-imposed and only through self-action can the mind be cleared.

Divinatory Meaning

Positive: A crisis situation has arisen over which the emotions have been allowed to rule. If any good is to result from the situation, detachment from the emotional wrongs or rights of the circumstances must occur.

Negative: Treacheries, or emotional hurts from the past still cloud the ability to think clearly. Trying to bend the will of others will only lead to emotional or mental breakdown.

Nine of Swords

A large full moon in the background, almost obscured by the figure in front, indicates emotional solitude and restrictions. The figure of a woman, her hands held up to her face in anguish, undergoes some form of mental torture while the surrounding swords destroy her. Her hair is entwined amongst the swords, making it even more difficult for her to break free from the anguish she clearly feels. The cosmos around her appears to swirl, as if a cold wind were blowing, yet she is alone upon the card symbolising her martyrdom, loneliness and unhappiness.

The nine of swords indicates that pain is a thing which one feels often only by oneself, however, this pain is self-inflicted as there are no other figures present. The card marks the obsessive and compulsive type of personality who acts before they think, then lives to regret the rashness of their decisions.

Divinatory Meaning

Positive: Anxiety for someone you love, a miscarriage of justice as you see it. Compulsive emotions which override the intellect.

Negative: You are under suspicion and know the level of your own guilt. It is too late for self-recrimination and you must pay the price for the mistakes you made, be they false loyalty to another or your own self-deception.

Ten of Swords

What was once a healthy tree now stands in ruins, its branches devoid of life impaled now with swords. From the swords blood runs, indicating the draining of the life forces while the large moon, symbolising the emotions, looks on in horror as the barren ground absorbs the very soul of the tree. This card is the indicator of mental death, or the giving up of mental abilities and responsibilities. It is however a living death as the swords have not cut deep enough to kill the tree, but appear to be bleeding it slowly of its last reserves of strength. The ten of swords is the indicator of mental exhaustion. The cycle of analysis and dissection of mental problems is over. Grief and sorrow at wrong decisions made have taken over.

Divinatory Meaning

Positive: Past failures bring desolation, grief and sorrow, ruin, pain, affliction and sadness for the dreams of what might have been, but failed to materialise.

Negative: The negative of this card is to avoid the pain and sorrow for a time, to reverse the situation and bring forth a victory where none thought it was possible. The victory, however, may only be momentary and other cards in proximity to this one must be read in order to come to a final interpretation.

Page of Swords

A young man stands on a mountain top amongst an abundance of flora. His feet are bare and he holds in his hands a sword pointing down into the ground. There is a blue rose in full bloom on the hilt. He is dressed to protect himself from the elements, yet appears overdressed for the weather conditions indicated. While he looks innocent and pure there is a hint that not all is as it should appear.

The blue rose in his hands indicates that he can manipulate the emotions of others, while his bare feet indicate that his nature is more animalistic than he would have us believe. The clouds behind indicate hidden secrets while the abundant flora a fertile imagination. The Page of Swords indicates a personality able to deceive and fool others with a discerning innocence. It indicates a grasp of the subtle uses of the mind to manipulate others and a sharp insight which can be concealed at will.

Divinatory Meaning

Positive: A person with the ability to perceive and conceal what others fail to notice. One who sees beyond the obvious and is adept at uncovering secrets.

Negative: An imposter, charlatan, or fake, who will adopt a false appearance to accomplish selfish desires.

Knight of Swords

The card shows a man in armour on a horse riding through a mist or storm cloud. His face appears determined and the sword, while resting over his left shoulder, could easily be brought into use should he so desire. His helmet is crowned with a blue circle indicating a connection with the element of Air, while the purple-blue colouring of the card is indicative of one who is mentally in charge of emotions and expresses determination when his mind is made up. The horse shows strength and courage equal to that of the knight, warning those in their path to step aside or be trampled. The knight steers the horse with his right hand indicating that he is in control of his own direction or destiny.

This card indicates a young, proud and ambitious person, domineering in nature, but who feels that justice is on their side, be they misguided or not. Do not cross or oppose this type of personality for what they cannot achieve by force of mind they will achieve through physical domination.

Divinatory Meaning

Positive: Bravery, skill and chivalry; the forces of good mustered against evil. Headlong rush into the unknown without fear. Good at heart, courageous, shrewd and sharp.

Negative: An impulsive and conceited fool. Downfall through a woman other than his own. Disputes and arguments.

Queen of Swords

The crowned figure of a queen sits upon a throne made from a whirlwind. She has control of the element of Air. In her right hand she holds a double-edged sword upright, indicating her power, while in the left she holds a blue rose indicating that she controls the balance between her emotions and her intellect. Her hair blows in a strong wind indicating the power of her intellect. Her robe is purple in both dark and light shades indicating her spirituality, while she wears the blue sphere and the winged insignias of her office in her crown and around her neck. This card is indicative of a sharp and quick-witted woman. One who has learned through hard lessons and experience and has sharpened her intellect. She may be a widow, or have suffered a loss, yet it is this which has strengthened her and given her the ability to guide others from making the same mistakes.

Divinatory Meaning

Positive: A person who may be sought out for advice and guidance. One who has suffered personal loss and sorrow; a situation calling for spiritual guidance.

Negative: A bitter and lonely woman who has slanderous intent. Evil-minded, desiring all to suffer from their own past mishaps and sorrows. A narrowminded and treacherous enemy, who should be avoided.

King of Swords

A king sits proudly upon a throne fashioned from a whirlwind. He has control of the element of Air and therefore of the intellect. In his left hand, he holds a dish with a blue rose embossed on it, from which a sylph or Air elemental steps, indicating the service that this element will provide at the king's bidding. In his right hand, he holds the double-edged sword, symbol of his justice and truth. His crown sports the blue sphere, symbol of his element of Air, while his belt of power is of gold, indicating the success of his life. His face appears pure and devoid of fear, yet ready to take on the expression of his judgement. Flowers flourish at his feet. He appears to hold the balance between the symbols in his hands, yet while one is clenched indicating his strength to take, the other is open as if in an offering.

This card indicates a mature and successful man who has the power to sit in judgement of others. He has a sharp intellect, though is suspicious of all things until he has weighed their worth. He is the judge and handles authority as if it were his right.

Divinatory Meaning

Positive: Justice shall be seen to be done, wrongs will be righted, but those who have broken the rules must face the consequences.

Negative: A dangerous and wicked personality that will pursue desires at all costs. Cruel and sadistic.

SUIT OF WANDS

Ace of Wands

The card depicts the red rose of Fire and energy with a strong, clenched fist clasping a single wand. The wand is upright, strong and powerful indicating the male aspects of nature in all their splendour. The cosmos in the background appears to have just been born from an enormous explosion, as if the wand had created the universe itself. This indicates that in order to create something new, sacrifices must be made and the old way discarded. Each of the aces represents a new beginning and creation. They are the bearers of light and life, but are also capable of exploding under their own powerful force. This applies particularly to the Ace of Wands, for it is ruled by Fire which can warm the hearth of a home or rage out of control, burning it to the ground. The Ace of Wands represents creativity, new enterprises and beginnings.

Divinatory Meaning

Positive: Gains, inheritances, or the beginning of new enterprises, schemes and projects. An inventive individual; good fortune to those who desire it.

Negative: A false start to a project or enterprise, or the cancellation of plans already laid. Someone who is easily vexed or distracted. Unrealised goals and objectives result from misdirected energies.

Two of Wands

The card depicts a man and a woman facing each other. Each holds a wand out in front, as if to say that they were right, or they were first. There is an air of defiance in their stance and in their features. They are standing on top of a globe representing the earth and each seeks domination over the other. Their fists are clenched as if suppressing some form of energy or anger. The base of each of the wands is for the woman a red rose, symbolising her energy for passion, while for the man the base is a white flower, symbolising the creative masculine energy. They desire to combine and share, yet one must make the first move if anything is to come of the situation.

The two of wands symbolises power and dominion as shown by the red and orange of the robes of the two figures. A battle of wills, emotions, ambitions and desires is to take place before action can be instigated.

Divinatory Meaning

Positive: A dominant personality with courage and fortitude. Equality in partnership. The ability to exercise power over others through strength of will.

Negative: Resentment and jealousy leading to aggression. Restraint caused by others.

Three of Wands

A young fair-haired man stands between two trees. In his left hand he holds one wand, while in his right are two. His expression and stature leads one to believe he is proud at some form of achievement or personal possession, while his red robe glows with pride and energy. Around his head, a halo of light indicates the inspiration and enlightenment which has led him through his trials. The card is the indicator of success through good management and the use of applied knowledge. It signifies that organiser who is able to accomplish even under stress and suggests a knowledge beyond that of the age of the young man depicted. The card is a symbol of the accomplishment of tasks that have reached satisfactory conclusions.

Divinatory Meaning

Positive: The ability to organise and apply positive energy to business ventures. The acquisition of financial reward.

Negative: Over-confidence in ventures could lead to a downfall. Help or assistance offered by others is of no use, as success must come through one's own application. Those that offer help may in fact have ulterior motives and be helping themselves. Guard against treachery.

Four of Wands

The card depicts a male and female child playing in a garden which is in full bloom. Four wands complete a structure, which comprises two upright wands with a cross bar being the third and the fourth forming a support. From the structure many ribbons hang from which the children swing and play. In the background a large orange sun shines, indicating the joy and happiness of the card's energy and the fertility brought to the garden. The structure in the card symbolises foundations laid, which have been brought to fruition. These are the dreams of youth, or childhood. The card symbolises a period of prosperity and joy, a time to rejoice at the fruits of one's labours.

Divinatory Meaning

Positive: The acquisition of new land, property or objects desired in the past. A period of social activity and pleasure, weddings, christenings and the like.

Negative: The negative of this card is never entirely negative. In this case, the reversed meaning is an indication of incomplete happiness, or a time when a rest may be taken from the pressures of life, with the knowledge that the threads of hard labour must once again be taken up. Tasks only three quarters accomplished; work still required before rest can take place.

Five of Wands

In the background is a shaded or subdued, angry-looking sun, while in the foreground five batons or wands form a grid with three vertical and two horizontal. The figure of a young man clings to the wands, symbolising his desire to hold on to that which is his, while another figure clings to him, symbolising the battle he must fight with negative forces. This is further expressed by the two grasping hands which appear from the bottom of the card attempting to shake his support, or dislodge him from his perch. The overall colour of the card indicates anger, although the young man's face is serene, as if he is unconcerned with the strife to come.

This card indicates tests to be surmounted and overcome, obstacles which must be dealt with in order to maintain the balance in one's life.

Divinatory Meaning

Positive: Success and material achievements have been accomplished, though the battles undergone in their acquisition have left mistrust of the intentions of others. Ambitions are not yet fully matured and further work must be done.

Negative: Carelessness with material possessions which may be lost to others. Caution is required.

Six of Wands

The card depicts a fair-haired young man with the solar energy at his back. In his left hand he holds one baton while three others stand and two lie before him. His robe is bright red indicating physical prowess and he wears a laurel wreath, indicating some victory or accomplishment. His proud stance and the batons laid at his feet would indicate that offerings or homage are being offered to appease him. This card is indicative of creative changes brought about through hard work. Rewards for achievements and accomplishments, hard work and labours of the past are being acknowledged in the present.

Divinatory Meaning

Positive: Well-earned success and recognition for works which have been accomplished. Ideas which have merit and are worthy of praise. Material and spiritual rewards for efforts made.

Negative: One who says they have accomplished much, but has in fact done little. The taking of credit for the accomplishments of another. Inconclusive or useless gains, which serve no true purpose. This card can also be indicative of unfulfilled romances, or attention bestowed upon someone unworthy of it, or who does not desire this attention. Falsity and deception of all kinds.

Seven of Wands

What appears to be a fireball or nova sun blasts out
energy and anger from the background while the figure of
a man stands ready to swing a baton held over his right
shoulder in his defence against six other batons in front
of him. The whole card emphasises strength and the
ability to succeed no matter how strong the opposition.
All that is required is the will and determination to do
so. The hair of the figure stands on end, charged with
static electricity and energy as he sweeps aside those who
would oppose his aims and ambitions. This card appears
in spreads when strong action is required to win the day.
It represents the need at times for individuality and the
need to be self-motivated.

Divinatory Meaning

Positive: The fight for what is rightly yours is just,
regardless of the supposed consequences. Self-assertion is
called upon for achievement of the aims and ambitions of
youth. Others trespass upon your property or business
and you must fight for yourself.

Negative: You destroy what you cannot possess, or fear
others may take from you. Inability to stand upon one's
own two feet and fight for what is yours by right or
through hard work. Ruination. Use and abuse by others
stronger than yourself. Anxiety and stress result from a
lack of conviction in both yourself and your
achievements.

Eight of Wands

A blazing ball coloured for both the Sun and Moon is positioned in the background symbolising the energies of the two luminaries, while a right hand, governing the physical side of man, bursts forth from a bunch of leaves and sprouts eight batons with force and energy behind them. It is as if a new flower was born instantaneously. The eight of batons symbolises the conversion of energy, or regeneration. The Sun and Moon indicate male and female energies or qualities pushed together at the same time creating either a great force of renewal, or one of hasty destruction. The conversion of positive circumstances into negative or negative into positive takes place. This card is highly phallic in nature and may appear in connection with romance and love affairs.

Divinatory Meaning

Positive: There can be sudden action, unexpected progress and swiftly moving activity in matters concerning the heart. Hasty decisions are not good in the long term and some reconsideration of current events should take place in case circumstances move quickly out of control.

Negative: Hasty actions and decisions cause arguments and quarrels. Harassment from others to act immediately.

Nine of Wands

The background storm clouds represent great energy and strength, while in the foreground we see a man who appears muscular and strong. He grips with both hands a wand, while all around him, like spokes in a wheel, sit the other eight, as if shielding or protecting him. The ninth wand that he is holding appears to have exploded in his face, turning him into one of the wands. The man and the wand stand as one. Yet they remain within the circle of other wands, as if they are holding themselves back in reserve for future necessary action. This card governs the recuperation process before action. It indicates great strength, collected in reserve before its release. The card may appear when friends or family are in hospital recovering from illness. It indicates conscious control of inner strength, leading to self-control of energies and thence to victory.

Divinatory Meaning

Positive: Strength and vitality are in reserve, ready to overcome obstacles and illnesses. Plans well laid avoid problems that beset others.

Negative: A physically low ebb; susceptibility to illness and stress. The will is weak and false advice may be followed.

Ten of Wands

The universal clouds and their colours indicate that oppressive or negative forces may be at hand. The figure lying on his back is holding nine wands in the air without too much effort, but the tenth is poised ready to strike or crush him. It has, however, not done so yet and remains hovering above him. This card has a twofold effect in that it warns those who attempt too much that they will bring about their own downfall. At the same time it indicates that others may have the breathing space they require to lay one task to rest and catch the last wand before it falls.

This card is the symbol of judgement of one's own actions, the completion of creative works which now must be presented to others for them to see their worth. Creativity is, however, appreciated by a minority rather than a majority and this can be a burden.

Divinatory Meaning

Positive: A creative task has reached its conclusion and is now at the point of judgement. Personal losses are required of those who fail to measure up to their own perception of themselves.

Negative: The attempt to move too quickly, to handle too much, or try too hard. Consequences must now be faced. Lack of moral commitment and the revealing of true worth to others. Lies uncovered.

Page of Wands

The card depicts an exceptionally fertile background, with a youth kneeling before a candle, which appears to be burnt in offering. The trees either side of the youth and to the rear, symbolise good and evil forces and the arch they form his passage through such tests, or the start of tests to come. The red rose he holds in his left hand symbolises his passions and loved ones who he wishes to meet with again. The wand in his right hand indicates the support he may lean upon to see him through his trials. The youthful face gazes down at the red rose indicating his love or longing for someone. This card often appears when a new love affair or romance is about to begin, or when those who have been parted from each other will reunite.

Divinatory Meaning

Positive: News of a lover, friend, or associate is imminent. Action is required now. Strangers with good intention may be encountered in the near future. Letters, or emissaries may bring welcomed social news. Loyal friends are there for support, should they be required.

Negative: Tempers and unstable emotional outbursts lose friends. Those whose nature you try to dominate will reject you. Gossip about others and face them later at your peril, for they will know the source of the gossip and your intentions.

Knight of Wands

The figure of a knight swathed in red energy charges forward, with a fiery and angry skyline in the background. He grasps the baton, or wand, which is his by right of conquest. He is about to hurl it into the grasp of another. His armour sports the symbols of the Fire element, revealing his nature, as his passions are quickly and easily aroused. He travels light and rejects the restraints that others may try to impose upon him. He is a warrior, active and alert, but prone to impetuous actions.

Sensual by nature, but quick to switch his passions from one task to another, he has little patience for those who wish to debate and plan, desiring to let his actions speak for him. This card may indicate those who may be called away at a moment's notice to defend our rights. The knight is on horseback and on a journey which has not yet reached its final conclusion. He is unlikely to stop in one place for long.

Divinatory Meaning

Positive: One who can act quickly and without warning. An impetuous person whose passions are easily roused. An alert and creative thinker who knows his own mind. A journey into the unknown and a desire for adventure.

Negative: A breakup or parting in relationships. Conflict. A jealous individual with great inner anger.

The Queen of Wands

The Queen of Wands is a stately figure. She sits upon a wand throne dressed in the red robes of her element. Her jewellery, however, is silver symbolising the feminine lunar influence over her passionate energy. In her right hand, she firmly holds the baton which expresses her energy for action and her ability to judge others, while in her left sits a red rose, indicating her sympathy and passion to see that right is done.

This card is an indicator of the warm and compassionate individual, who helps and advises those who cannot see the course of life clearly. She is compassionate and ready to give advice, but just as capable of delivering a truthful blow if that is what is required. Her motives are unselfish and this is expressed by the personal sacrifices she makes on behalf of others.

Divinatory Meaning

Positive: A person who inspires others by the examples they set. A teacher, a mother, a warm and affectionate person, who inspires emulation. A person with strong virtues, chaste and affectionate, but determined.

Negative: One who appears virtuous, but uses treachery and guile to get their own way. One who is untrustworthy and wriggles out of commitments made.

King of Wands

The magnificent figure of a bearded man sits upon a throne of batons. His stature pours forth pride and magnetism and inspires trust in the decisions he makes. In his left hand, he holds a gold dish with the emblem of the red rose and in the dish sits a salamander. In his right hand, he holds his wand and the balance of his judgement is made through his own self-sacrifice. Upon his head is his red triangle of power while about his waist a gold belt, both emblems of authority.

This card is the indicator of the maturer, stronger and courageous person, passionate in their beliefs and at times even hasty, but always ready to put right any wrong they may have done. The King of Wands is admired and is a magnetic personality and often an indictator of a good lover. This card may indicate that passions and courage are the order of the day and that good will triumph over evil.

Divinatory Meaning

Positive: An educated, conscientious and friendly person. A mature person regardless of age. A devoted friend, husband, or lover. A sympathetic person who will lend a hand, a father figure to see you through your problems.

Negative: A rigid, old-fashioned and dogmatic individual, who is trapped in the ideology of the past. One who may blame others for lost opportunities.

SUIT OF CUPS

Ace of Cups

A bright cosmic dawn springs forth the white rose from which stems a hand holding a golden chalice. The cup is overflowing and water, the elemental ruler of this suit, flows out of the cup from four corners. This symbolises the overflowing emotional capability of this card, though also warns that too much may drown those who drink from it. From the top of the cup the emblem consisting of a white dove, expressing purity, and a cross upon a white disc, indicating peace, protrudes. This card appears when emotional renewal, or assistance, is required. It is an indicator of those who are emotionally loyal, faithful and available in times of need.

Divinatory Meaning

Positive: Love, joy, fertility and renewal. Inspiration and spiritual elevation are indicated for the future. New love, romance, or kindred spirits. The beginning of new artistic projects.

Negative: Emotional upsets and upheaval. Loss of faith in oneself, or those close to the heart. Barrenness of feeling, unhappiness, depression, or the loss of a woman close to your heart.

Two of Cups

The card depicts a couple standing arm in arm holding overflowing cups. The branches of the trees form a halo above them and the peace, love and contentment that the card represents, ooze from every corner. This card signifies emotional partnerships based on strong friendship, mutual feelings and understanding. It expresses cooperation between the emotional forces of masculinity and femininity. It often appears to represent those who have been happily married for many years, or those who are about to enter marriage. Even in friendship, this card's energy has that extra bit of loving which the other 'twos' fail to match.

Divinatory Meaning

Positive: The perfect, understanding partner. Emotional attunement with those you love. Friendships which are deep and meaningful. Renewed passions, second honeymoons, love and romance which blooms.

Negative: Too much emotional intensity which a partner is unable to cope with. Separation, divorce, divisions brought about through falsity of expression. Troubled relationships which are not being emotionally expressed. Opposition to a romance from others not directly involved.

Three of Cups

A woman appears to dance upon turbulent waters or even to have parted the waves. In front of her feet rests an overflowing cup, while she holds another in each hand. The turbulent waters here indicate excited or stressed emotions, while the full cups show that the figure has the strength to overcome any emotional obstacles placed before her. She smiles in the face of adversity, because her emotions are strong and she knows she will overcome any danger. This is the card which signifies abundance. It emphasises that good luck and health are on your side and that emotional endeavours are being recognised and will be justly rewarded. The efforts made in the past at last find appreciation.

Divinatory Meaning

Positive: The resolution of emotional problems. Compromises have been made. Healing energy for both yourself and those who seek you out. Rewards for emotional energies expended on others, with full recognition for time, patience and effort.

Negative: Pain and stress brought upon by overindulgence. Excessive pleasure leading to illness. The loss of prestige in the eyes of others through emotional gluttony. Unrecognised ability left to waste.

Four of Cups

The card depicts a rocky outcrop on a moonlit night from which a waterfall cascades. Four golden cups appear under the waterfall and from each blooms a white rose. One cup is in front of the other three and held by a hand as if in offering. The waterfall symbolises cascading emotions while the four cups represent firm foundations, though the fact that the moon rises within the top of the waterfall and that the water drops to crash on the base of the cliff, are indicators that the emotions are of an inconsistent nature. The clouded base to the cliff is hidden leaving doubt as to the firmness of the foundations. This card indicates that emotions alone build weak foundations, that familiarity breeds contempt and that the element Water may feed Earth, but can erode it and wash it away.

Divinatory Meaning

Positive: New possibilities, new approaches to old problems. New acquaintances and friendships. A refusal to base decisions upon emotions alone.

Negative: Weariness and boredom. Disappointments and unhappiness. Failure to be content with what you have, or lack of appreciation of what others may offer or grant as a gift. Weak emotional foundations in personal relationships lead to a breakdown in communication.

Five of Cups

The figure of a woman stands in the foamy, unsettled waves of the sea. The moon lights her way and she empties the contents of two cups into the waters. Her hair is swept by the wind and, while two other cups appear empty, the fifth contains a white rose in bloom, which she has not yet noticed. The green robe indicates fertility, yet she appears sad, as if from a loss. The empty cups reveal her emotional loss, but the blooming cup she has not noticed will show her that sacrifice will be well rewarded. She should be full of hope for the future, yet sees only the gloom of present circumstances. This card may appear when dreams are taking too long to fulfil, or family life appears to be on a downward tack. Hope is there. It has only to be recognised.

Divinatory Meaning

Positive: Sacrifices made and pleasures missed have been noted and the future will see things brought into balance, with patience. Current loves may not be right, but the right one is not too far away. Those missed will return soon.

Negative: Friendship without meaning; marriages without love. Flaws in relationships. The loss of someone loved. Hobbies or dreams which are beyond reach at this time.

Six of Cups

The figure of a woman sits upon the crest of a wave and is supported by it, representing her emotional support. In her right hand she holds a white rose in bloom while her left grips the cup at the top of the pyramid of six cups, also containing a white rose, as do the others below it. She is offering the cups full of emotional purity, with the extra rose held in reserve for those who should have need of it. This card symbolises the need for emotional adjustments, which must be made if wishes are to be fulfilled. A purification of motives and ideals for future development and security is required.

Divinatory Meaning

Positive: The present and its potential opportunities are at a point when decisions must be made. The planned future needs to be revised and redirected, or there may be failure to live up to expectations. Success and help is being offered, but it involves a change of direction.

Negative: Living in the memories and nostalgia of the past may set the trap of an emotional rut. Things which have vanished from life, but have not been released, affecting future projects and desires.

Seven of Cups

A young, forlorn youth grasps at as many cups as he can hold, while hands reach out trying to loose his hold upon them. Behind him the figure of a female, her face changing from a smile to a look of contempt or disappointment, watches over what is happening. She holds two cups, the one in her left hand as in an offering, with a moon rising from it, while the one in her right is firmly grasped. These two cups symbolise the desire to give, but there are forces which prevent this. It is the effect of the dreamer and self-deceiver, who fails to trust the emotional motives of others. The lesson the card teaches is that emotional reality must be accepted and that dreams have no place here. What appears to be brown smoke depicted on this card is the clue to a blindness that can cloud the emotions.

Divinatory Meaning

Positive: Desire, determination and willpower will see that what was due will be attained. An emotional goal is nearing fulfilment. Do not give in now. You have made the right choice and should stick to your guns.

Negative: Fear of failure clouds vision. Foolish whims and self-delusion block the path. Fantasy and reality must be overcome and trust must be placed in others.

Eight of Cups

The figure of a woman sits with a look of madness on her face, her hair blown to the wind. Above her rests a full moon indicting an emotional ending, while she appears to be about to cast a basket with eight cups upon the ocean, as if to be rid of something, or trusting to fate alone. This card indicates emotional dissatisfaction. The need for regeneration is at hand and all that prevents this, or is no longer of any use, must be cast aside, or thrown away. The card may indicate dissatisfaction with the way children have turned out, lovers may not be as we dreamed they would be, or ambitions as important as we had first thought.

Divinatory Meaning

Positive: Effort will be continued until dreams are realised and wishes fulfilled. The old way will be discarded in order that the new may be born. A celebration to end the old and begin the new.

Negative: Effort required to make plans a reality is not made. Lost hope and failure. Others have disappointed you with their efforts and you now realise that you must detach yourself from them. Abandonment of what could have been a successful project, through shyness, modesty, or a fear of failure.

Nine of Cups

In the background is a full moon from which the happy and smiling faces of a man and woman shine forth. Below them lie nine cups from each of which blooms a white rose of purity, or emotional contentment. Amongst the cups sits the figure of a woman, her hair intertwined with the moon and the hair of the faces reflected in it indicating her emotional harmony and contentment. The card indicates that emotional consciousness (moon) coupled with material energy (earth) will lead to material gain and success.

This card is often called the 'wish granted' card and has its equivalent in playing cards in the nine of hearts. All obstacles can be surmounted and when this card appears, it neutralises even the negative effects of major arcana cards. Its own negative effects relate to delays, rather than failure.

Divinatory Meaning

Positive: Success and material advancement. Good health. Advancement, or promotion for effort. A period where it seems you just can't put a foot wrong. A wish granted.

Negative: Manipulation of others can cause delays in progress. Material possessions owed, or money which others delay payment of. A false sense of security can lead to overcommitment.

Ten of Cups

Two hands reach out from a moon offering success and joy in the form of ten cups, in two rows of five. Each chalice, or cup, contains a sacred rose in red (energy), blue (emotion), gold (attainment) and white (purity). At the base of the cups, within the hands, is a larger, white rose, indicating the purity and completeness of that which is being offered, while the whole cosmos is alight with their energy.

This card is the indicator of emotional maturity and completeness and indicates that health, wealth and happiness are yours. It reveals that a period of growth has reached an end and that peace of mind is at last here on earth. Spirituality can now be obtained.

Divinatory Meaning

Positive: Happiness at home and work. Pleasure and contentment in all environments. A good family life, with both a love for and a love from others bringing esteem, joy and contentment.

Negative: Loss of friends, family members, or those close to the heart. Opposition, or differences of opinion with those you love. Petty family disputes and quarrels, which you would rather were not there. Anger, dischord, or unhappiness, which lowers resistance to sickness.

Page of Cups

A young man stands on what appears to be either a carpet, or pyramid of flowers, which appears to give him passage through a sea of waves. In his right hand, a chalice, or cup, sparkles, while in his left he holds a white rose upon a purple velvet cushion, as if he revered its presence. The symbolism combines to indicate a spiritual and pure-minded youth, fair-haired and blue-eyed. He is as yet untainted by the emotional insecurities of adulthood, full of trust in his fellow man, a trust he inspires in others by his presence. He is a Good Samaritan to those in need, thoughtful of the needs of others and ready to be of service when he can. He is artistic and cultured and brings refinement into the lives of those he meets.

Divinatory Meaning

Positive: A studious and intense personality. A person willing to be of assistance and to apply effort to specific goals. Meditative and loyal to those they meet. A bearer of news. One who is gifted in music or the arts. A creative person.

Negative: A flatterer, who easily distracts one from true objectives. A selfish individual, who thinks only of themselves. A deceiver and liar who believes in their own fairytales.

Knight of Cups

The moon shines through a break in the clouds, indicating emotional insight, while the figure of a knight kneels in full armour beside his horse, which grazes peacefully upon a white rose. The knight offers up an overflowing chalice, or cup, of emotions, symbolising his willingness to be of service, yet he is dismounted and not prepared for battle. Both he and the horse wear the symbols of the moon, stressing the presence of emotional energies. This card is indicative of the dreamer, the knight in shining armour, who will do good deeds and rid the earth of its evils. While his desire to help may be genuine, his horse, so well fed, is unlikely to be ready to gallop into the fray. The white rose in the knight's right hand, on his material side, is also an indicator that he is a lover rather than the fighter he would have you believe in.

Divinatory Meaning

Positive: A sensitive and imaginative individual, who is a born dreamer and a romantic. A proposal, invitation, or inducement may soon be offered. Opportunities, which may or may not materialise.

Negative: A sly and cunning individual who will twist emotions to suit his own ends. A trickster, who may run off with more than a broken heart. Any situation pertaining to vice or drugs.

Queen of Cups

A resplendent figure of a woman sits on a throne made from a waterfall. From beneath her feet spring forth forms of growth, while in her right hand she holds the chalice of intuition. In her left hand is the white rose of purity. She wears the symbols of her power, the crescent moon crown and the fish, on a string of pearls. Her chalice is covered, for her intuition is a guarded secret and the richness of her robes shows she is willing to share her intuition with those who attempt to understand its effect. This card symbolises psychic and intuitive forces at play, the mother, who is emotionally and psychically in touch with cosmic forces.

Divinatory Meaning

Positive: Remember your dreams for they may hold psychic messages, or at least some form of advice or guidance. A devoted wife or mother. A sensitive fair-haired female, who has feelings for you.

Negative: False dreams and impressions, which should be avoided as they lead to self-treachery. Psychic energies out of balance, requiring meditation to readjust them. A deceitful, fair-haired woman. Falsity and deception are pitting their forces against you. Beware of selfishness and jealousy.

King of Cups

As with the queen, the throne is that of a waterfall, though for the King of Cups, the chalice held in his right hand is open. In his left hand, he holds a water elemental, an undine, who will do his bidding with pleasure. The undine sits in a golden bowl, which bears his seal of the white rose. His beard is long, like that of an old man, while he is in fact still young. He has emotional understanding and knowledge. He is the silent type, quiet and strong, with no need to prove himself. He is a student of human nature, a philosopher and scientist, but in addition he has the extra ability of the intuitive, or psychic. He is a man who acts when necessary and then always decisively.

Divinatory Meaning

Positive: A creative thinker, or learned individual. A considerate person, slow to anger, but unstoppable if aroused. A man interested in the intuitive sciences. Powers not displayed, but held in reserve. The father figure.

Negative: Injustice, deceit and trickery. Scandal. One who uses intuition for his own ends. The black magician. A forger, or double dealer.

SUIT OF PENTACLES

Ace of Coins or Pentacles

The card depicts a right hand bursting forth from a gold rose. The hand holds a single, large pentacle, or coin. All around the base of the pentacle are berries and leaves and it appears to shimmer and shine in the cosmic background. The gold rose is the elemental symbol of earth, while the berries and leaves indicate the fertility of the earth and mother nature's rewards to those who make use of her energies. The shining effect of the pentacle indicates achievements and possibilities realised, so when this card appears, some form of material gain has or will soon be made.

Divinatory Meaning

Positive: Completion, perfection and attainment. Great wealth in relationship to the environment. Good luck and a lucky omen for gamblers. A period of prosperity, where the work of the past may at last be harvested in material terms. A happy, stable and contented period.

Negative: Prosperity, though without the joy it could bring. Wealth without love. Ambitions fulfilled in the material realm, though too late to save the emotional. Wasted money and misused wealth. Money obtained through corruption, falsity and deceit, which will bring no happiness or joy.

Two of Pentacles

Under the arch of two great trees stand the figures of a
man and a woman. They stand back to back and lean
upon each other for support and each holds a pentacle,
which appears to be linked to the other through some
form of energy flow. There are two conclusions to be
drawn here. Either that each works well in harmony with
the other, or that each is too busy with their own energy
to notice the needs of the other. The way this card is
perceived is the indicator of its positive or negative
effects. The card itself suggests partnerships and a need
for balance between the masculine and feminine qualities
for real success. One out of balance with the other will
affect the energy flow and lessen the harmony of the
relationship.

Divinatory Meaning

Positive: The ability to harmonise situations, to handle
others and adjudicate in disputes. A letter, or news from
a loved one, who is far away from home. You would
work better with a partner than you ever have by
yourself.

Negative: Difficulty in launching new projects and
enterprises. Embarrassment brought on by the actions of
a partner. Worry, or concern in how things are
developing within partnerships. Monetary worries
brought about by a careless partner, or spouse.

Three of Pentacles

A young man stands in the foreground with tools in his hands. He appears well-dressed and pleased with himself and the work he has done in engraving the three pentacles upon the branches of the two trees, which stand behind him. This is the card of the craftsman, who has worked hard to become the master of his trade. It indicates work with materials, which requires skill and dexterity. It states that those who show these qualities will be suitably rewarded.

Divinatory Meaning

Positive: A craftsman. One who works with great skill and dexterity. A situation handled with skill and diplomacy. Artistic ability at work. Dignity, wealth and power, which come from hard work and the mastery of an art. New projects which, if mastered, bring great rewards to those who make the effort.

Negative: A wasted skill put to misuse. Mediocre and sloppy work, which is unacceptable and below capabilities. Lack of effort. Common ideas, which are thought to be special or gifted. Over opinionated self-esteem, which has yet to be earned. Worry over money matters, which will require hard work to solve.

Four of Pentacles

A young man playing at being king of the castle, or mountain, stands on top of four pentacles. He has a look of pride or achievement about him and on his chest the gold rose of earthly attainments shines forth. Strong, interwoven branches form a canopy over his head and the greenery at his feet indicates the fertility of his foundations. The four pentacles also shine and are linked together in a box, or square formation, which indicates that firm foundations bring forth success and stability and a reason to be proud of tasks accomplished. This card signifies material foundations well laid and the first step on the road to success. Plans well laid and followed through lead to material gain.

Divinatory Meaning

Positive: You have achieved the foundations from which you may set forth upon quests with the knowledge of a secure material base. Status, power and glory are the things of your dreams and these can now be achieved, if you continue in the present direction. Accomplishment, monetary gain and career achievement.

Negative: Squandering of money and opportunities, which have been worked hard for. Ruin, unless plans are rethought. Setbacks in material shares or holdings. Others oppose the acquiring of further material gain.

Five of Pentacles

In the cosmic background appear five golden roses indicating magical or illusionary forces at play. The figure of a man who is either a beggar or a hermit, garbed in a robe with a staff in his right hand, reaches out for a gold rose of absolute achievement. The staff indicates that he is supported by materialism, while his blue scarf shows the imagination at play. Is the rose a pot of gold which he may carry away, or a flower which will wilt and die when plucked from the earth?

This card shows both poverty and the possibility of wealth and indicates one who learns through the failures of the past. Those who see only the gold bring about their own destruction, while those who see the flower as a thing of beauty have the ability to overcome obstacles and survive.

Divinatory Meaning

Positive: The reversal of a bad trend or situation. Money from unexpected sources to solve financial worries. New expression in a partnership or marriage averting its ruin. One who sees the error of their ways and can begin anew.

Negative: Material insecurity leading to greed and ruin. Broken marriages and romances. Business ventures which were an error. Loneliness, poverty and self-delusion.

Six of Pentacles

Three pentacles appear at the top and the bottom of the card while an orb of the world hangs in the middle on a frame, as though it were the balance in a set of scales. This is further emphasised by the dishes that some of the pentacles appear to rest in. On either side a hand also appears and while one seems to direct, the other makes fine adjustments, as if bringing into being a more exact state of balance.

The images represent the fine attunement of financial resources resulting in material gains or success. Helping hands are at work here. The card symbolises the sharing of those resources in the form of charity, generosity and the giving of gifts. It shows one who is prepared to give a helping hand to those not so well off.

Divinatory Meaning

Positive: Material gain puts the enquirer in the position of being a benefactor to those less well off. A generous and well-meaning person. Kindness and sincerity. A balance between personal, material needs and those of loved ones. The reallocation of funds, which brings success.

Negative: Selfish and self-centred ideals cause meanness with financial resources. Debts owed, which remain unpaid. One who uses financial bribes to bring about their desires. An ungiving and mean individual, who counts only their own needs.

Seven of Pentacles

A blazing sun appears in the background under which a young man sows seeds from a green sack. All around him buds appear in the foliage and he treads on the ground in bare feet. The green sack shows he has the ingredients for growth, while the budding plants show that he must work to plant and nurture his ideas if he is to reap their harvest. The sun gives him this energy and warmth but only if he sows his seeds.

This card indicates ideas born which require work and application if they are ever to be brought to fruition. It also suggests the ingenuity to know where to plant the seed, the patience to care for it while it grows and the hard work to reap the final harvest. Time must pass and conditions or obstacles be overcome before any completion can take place.

Divinatory Meaning

Positive: Treasure and gain through hard efforts and perseverance. A successful and well-executed plan or idea which brings financial rewards. Hard work, but growth and an end are in sight.

Negative: Impatience at completing tasks means not enough attention is paid to detail. An unwise investment in time, energies and monetary fields of endeavour. Worry and anxiety over material investments as yet unproven.

Eight of Pentacles

A sun is either setting or rising in the distance while a tree in full fruit, represented by the six pentacles in its branches, grows in front of it. Before the tree kneels the figure of a young farmer, who is planting a pentacle into the ground, while another waits to be planted. The young man looks pleased with the work he is about to complete.

This card represents regeneration, the young man has taken some of the fruit of the tree and is replanting it in order that a further harvest may be gained. Yet the tree still has enough fruits (pentacles) to sustain any needs he may have now. The card indicates that his past skill has borne its fruits and he would do well to follow the skills he knows are successful for his future benefits.

Divinatory Meaning

Positive: Personal effort brings its own rewards. Old tried and tested methods are best in the present circumstances. A job well done, a harvest gathered in, prudent planning for the future years. An apprenticeship well learned.

Negative: Lack of ambition, misuse of given or taught crafts or abilities. Dissillusion at being trapped in the present circumstances. Badly planted crops which will bear no fruit. More risks are required to achieve aims.

Nine of Pentacles

A woman of beauty and grace, her hair flowing and full of blooms, waters her garden. She is as Mother Nature, giving life-generating liquids back to the earth, in order that she may reap its rewards. Her breasts are full, indicating her fertility, while about her neck she wears a shining string of pearls linking her into the energies of the major arcana card, the Empress.

This card expresses the conscious use of knowledge to bring about material gain, or success. The figure is feminine, symbolising the fertile female rather than the male hunter. Her presence brings about a feeling of well-being and caring even to the degree of luxury.

Divinatory Meaning

Positive: Comfort, safety and fulfilment through the efforts of the past. A love of nature, its plants and creatures. Foresight leaving one well cared for in old age. Personal hobbies and interests and the ability to nurture them. Material well-being, love and fortitude.

Negative: Bad faith, or lack of trust in others can bring self-fulfilling upsets. Lack of love, trust and understanding has caused a split home or lost friendship. The loss, or theft of treasured possessions. Danger of theft and loss through careless attention to things loved. Taking others for granted.

Ten of Pentacles

From out of the cosmos appears a cornucopia, or 'horn of plenty'. Part of its contents are the ten pentacles at the front. A solar energy representing material fulfilment illuminates the scene, while the green/orange background represents the fertility and energy of the card.

This card is the significator of material completion and worldly success. It signifies safe retirement with plenty of comfort, an inheritance in terms of money, or gifts and skills. It is the card of abundance and security at any age.

Divinatory Meaning

Positive: Prosperous and successful ambitions and aims. A nest egg for retirement. A redundancy payment, or compensation for ills and injuries. An inheritance of land, property, or ability. Material security and a reaping of harvest for work completed.

Negative: Troubles with finances in old age, and worry about how to make ends meet. Coveting the wealth or possessions of others, who have worked harder than you. Gamblers who rely too much on chance and not enough on good planning. Tax or revenues which have been avoided and may catch you out.

Page of Pentacles

A starlit scene with two trees forming pillars and an arch with a mountain range between are in the backround, from which a carpet of flowers stretches over the empty void. Here, before a golden rose of achievement, which grows between his feet, stands a daintily dressed youth. He gazes between his hands where he holds a pentacle and symbol of his elemental existence. The mountains and parted trees symbolise the hardships of a journey, while the carpet of flowers shows its worth.

The card signifies hard work and quests in search of knowledge and growth or maturity. It indicates a hard worker, who applies himself to a task and its hardships in order that he may create anew from the lessons or teachings of their research.

Divinatory Meaning

Positive: Deep concentration and research bring solutions as yet uncovered. Study, scholarship and reflection bring a thirst for knowledge and what it can achieve. Mind over matter, mental energy over physical power. New ideas and new opinions.

Negative: A failure to recognise the obvious. Unrealistic views and opinions which do not fit into the present situation. Circumstances beyond the control of the individual. An unrealistic person.

Knight of Pentacles

The figure of a young knight stands in a forest. His horse affectionately attends him revealing their companionship. The knight's horse is adorned with the flowers of nature, while the knight kneels in contemplation of the beauty which surrounds him. Both the knight and his horse wear the symbols of Earth, the pentacle and the square and the sheild of the knight forms a large pentacle showing that earth forces watch over him

This card depicts a person who is the 'salt of the earth', one who is mature, dependable and reliable. It is the symbol of truth in oneself and others and the methodical and practical application of earthly forces. It is a significant indicator of one who is now capable of responsibility.

Divinatory Meaning

Positive: The ability to complete the task at hand. Maturity brings responsibility. One who has done much and reflects upon the experiences it has given, in order that they may be put to future good use. A persistent and patient individual who bides his time.

Negative: Limitation brought about by dogmatic views and ideals. Failure brought about by shortcomings. Inability to put lessons learned to constructive useage. Lack of direction, or determination.

Queen of Pentacles

A throne of green leaves upon which sits the figure of a young queen is depicted. A gold cube, symbol of earth energy and indicator of the knowledge she possesses rests upon her head, while in her left hand she holds the gold rose of material success. In her right hand is a pentacle. Her jewellery is silver, in contrast to the gold of the cube. This symbolises her intuitive links with the earth and nature. She appears as though about to rejoice or announce a proclamation.

This card signifies a mature woman who has brought spiritual values to a material level. A tower of strength, warm-hearted and compassionate, she can rise above material matters, yet still keep her feet firmly on the ground.

Divinatory Meaning

Positive: A happy marriage or partnership, built upon firm foundations and spiritual compatibility. A mother, or wife and all they represent. Extreme comfort can be obtained, or great wealth acquired, through a female of this type. A generous female benefactor.

Negative: A person who pretends to have more than they do. A woman who lives beyond her means at the expense of others. Someone who will marry for money or material gain. Someone who hides unhappiness by spending money.

King of Pentacles

The figure of a man with a magnetic personality and who inspires confidence sits upon his earthly throne of leaves. In his right hand he holds a pentacle, while in his left sits a troll, gnome, or Earth elemental, ready to do his bidding. The gnome sits on a golden dish which bears his earthly seal of power, the golden rose. His head has the golden square upon it as does his queen, though he also wears a belt made from the same cubes. This is his belt of power. On closer inspection, we see that the gnome smokes a pipe. The king appears to be weighing the balance between the use of the gnome or using the energy of the pentacle.

This card denotes a mature and powerful man who knows how to weigh the consequences of his actions and moves only when he is certain of success. It shows good judgement in business matters and the ability to discriminate between right and wrong.

Divinatory Meaning

Positive: A manager, a leader, capable in everyday matters. A good advisor, one with much knowledge and worldly experience. A person of good character, a loyal friend. Business acumen and mathematical/scientific ability.

Negative: One who will use any means to acquire his ends. An unfaithful husband or business partner.

NUMBERS ON THE CARDS

Having described the symbolism represented by each card, which was considered individually, the next step is to learn to judge their interaction with each other. Before doing this, however, it is useful in interpretation to realise that the numbers of the cards offer clues as to the meaning that they express and it is with this in mind that the following short interpretations are offered.

Aces or One Cards

The ones symbolise new beginnings. They are ruled by the Sun and solar energy can either warm the soil and bring forth new life, or burn it into a wasteland. Ones denote new enterprises, or achievements through creativity.

Two Cards

The two cards all denote partnerships and the interaction between the male and the female energies. Twos are ruled by the Moon and therefore represent intuition and are linked strongly with the psychic arts, as well as with the emotions.

Three Cards

The threes are ruled by Mercury and denote goals to be achieved and endeavours to be undertaken. They govern the intellect, or mind, giving free will and choice to those who utilise their energies positively.

Four Cards

The fours are ruled by Jupiter and represent the philosophers who create the building blocks of our society. They symbolise firm foundations, consolidation and the correct application of the four elements to create spiritual energies and awareness.

Five Cards

The fives are ruled by Mars and represent the energy which motivates us. They denote the purpose of our actions and that which motivated us to be as we are. They represent the energies behind our actions.

Six Cards

The six cards are ruled by the planet Venus and govern feelings of love and our emotional reactions and interactions with others. Adaptability and the ability to accept changes within our lives are represented by the sixes.

Seven Cards

The seven cards are ruled by the planet Saturn and govern tests to be undergone and lessons which have to be learned to promote our spiritual and material evolution. They show what must change to bring growth.

Eight Cards

The eight cards are ruled by the polar force of masculinity and femininity or positive and negative energy and the balances which must be achieved between the two. The conversion of one type of energy to another and regeneration in general are represented by the eights.

Nine Cards

The nine cards are also governed by Saturn, but relate more to our consciousness, while Jupiter's influence in addition indicates the need for expansion. These are the cards of give and take, or the application of developed knowledge in a successful manner.

Ten Cards

Finally, we come to the ten cards which relate to the Sun and the Moon. They represent completion and the combining of these two energies into a unity. They deal with the unification of opposites, the bringing together of enemies and the balance required for peace and rest.

SPREADS TO TRY

We are now in a position to spread the cards and interpret them as a whole. Three types of spread will be described. It is a good idea to try each of them in order to discover which suits your own personality and approach to interpretation.

The first to be dealt with is the *Celtic Cross*. This spread has clearly defined card positions for expressing the energy of individual cards and is an excellent spread for answering specific questions.

The second spread to be described is the *Astrology Spread*. This spread channels the energy of the cards through specific 'house' positions. Each house represents an area of life which can be easily understood and interpreted in terms of everyday circumstances. The interpretation of this spread can then be projected into the future or the past as desired giving a wider means of understanding.

The final spread is that of the *Six Card Spread*. Less used by tarot readers than the others, it is however excellent for quick and accurate assessment of situations, or for answering questions.

There are many other methods of laying the cards and many tarot readers later develop their own versions. It is hoped that the three to be described will provide a firm foundation on which to build initial confidence and skill in interpretation.

1

THE
CELTIC CROSS

For this spread a 'significator' must first be chosen. A
significator is simply one of the 78 cards which governs
the question or situation under scrutiny. Let us say it
was desired to discover if a woman was to become
pregnant in the coming year. An excellent major arcana
card to select as significator would be the Empress, as
she symbolises birth and renewal. This card is then
removed from the pack and placed upon the surface
being used to do the consultation. The remaining cards
are given to the questioner to shuffle while he or she
concentrates upon the question. The cards are then
returned to the reader, can be further cut and then laid
out in the following order as shown on the next page.

Card number one placed on top of the significator,
indicates the essence of the situation, governing the
question asked, while card number two, which crosses it,
indicates any opposition or obstacle which must be dealt
with. Card three indicates the roots or background to the
question asked, while card four in conjunction will
describe the recent past, or what has brought the
questioner to their current situation. Card five indicates
possible outcomes or the expression of hopes and
aspirations, while card six read in conjunction will
indicate the near future, the outcome or probability of
success or failure.

The final four cards which are positioned in a column
on the right of the spread are supporting or contributing
factors to whatever has already been determined. Seven

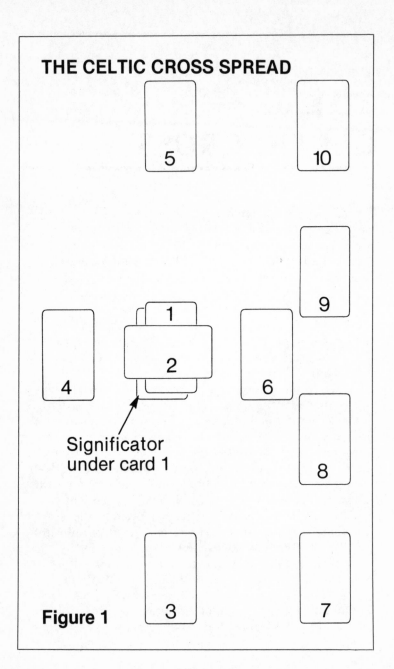

THE CELTIC CROSS SPREAD

5

10

1

2

4

6

9

8

Significator
under card 1

3

7

Figure 1

114

indicates the desired outcome, while card eight reveals the environment, or people which will affect the outcome or wishes of the questioner. Card nine indicates the hopes and fears which may transpire, while the final card in position ten is the prediction card, for it shows the eventual outcome. It should never be read in isolation for it is governed by that which passed before it.

Some tarot readers make a ritual out of the laying of this spread. It is not necessary, but if you wish to follow this path, when you cover the significator with card one, say "This covers you". When card two is laid, say "This crosses you". When card three is laid, say "This is below you" and with card four, say "This is behind you". When card five is laid, say "This crowns you" and with card six, say "This is before you". When card seven is laid, say "Your hopes and wishes" and with card eight, say "The wishes of those around you". When card nine is laid, say "The probable outcome" and with card ten, say "The conclusion, or outcome".

It may be helpful to make a layout sheet like the diagram on a board or piece of cloth to help lay the cards in the correct order each time.

Having now dealt with the method of laying the Celtic Cross, let us consider a sample reading.

Sample Reading using the Celtic Cross

Question asked: Will I become pregnant this year?
Significator chosen: The Empress
Spread as follows.

Card 1	Ten of Batons
Card 2	Eight of Batons
Card 3	King of Cups
Card 4	Wheel of Fortune
Card 5	Two of Swords
Card 6	The World
Card 7	Eight of Swords
Card 8	The Chariot
Card 9	Six of Cups
Card 10	Four of Swords

These were the cards as they fell and were placed in their correct positions according to the Celtic Cross spread on page 114. The card covering depicts a message of living up to the creative nature in oneself which may be under some form of pressure in the form of judgement from others. The obstacles, or crossing card the Eight of Batons, governs the coming together of Sun and Moon, positive and negative, to form regeneration. This immediately suggests that the questioner is under pressure from others to accomplish the task at hand rather than it being simply her own wish.

Looking now to card three governing the basis for her question and card four the recent past, we find that the King of Cups and Wheel of Fortune are brought into play. The Wheel of Fortune is usually a positive force, but only after a trial. The King of Cups can be a generous and kindly man who always has a hidden intuition or reserve of energy at his disposal. These factors guide the reader to look at card eight for environmental effects and here lies the key to cards three and four and their expression through the Eight of Swords. This card indicates the inability to see beyond the situation at hand and shows mental pressure is being applied to the circumstances. I questioned my client as to whether or not she wanted a child now or was she being pressured by others to do so before she is fully ready. I also tried to uncover why she was mentally unprepared at this time. Clues to this lie in both cards five and six and card eight. Cards five and six indicate the immediate future and the possible development of the situation and the Two of Swords here indicates that differences must be reconciled before the future event can transpire. The World indicates that this is possible and new growth can appear though not too soon as it is opposite the Wheel of Fortune. The Chariot in the eighth card position indicates success and victory and the true support of friends and associates though at present there are forces in opposition. The Six of Cups in position nine indicates dreams can now be fulfilled but mature people must make their own decisions. The final outcome card in position ten, the Four of Swords, clearly indicates the need for a rest from a battle or effort.

The choice to make here is will the rest come through the success of becoming pregnant or does the rest occur because the pressure to become pregnant eases and a decision is made to put the event off until a future, mutually agreeable date? I decided it was the latter and put it to my client that she felt pressured by those around her to have children now when she would rather continue in her career. I suggested that if she was to discuss it with her mate they would be able to make suitable arrangements for a family which both felt able to deal with in the future rather than being tied down by children now. She answered me saying that her husband wanted children now and that she had been unable to tell him that she was not agreeable because of financial commitments and a desire to carry on working.

She subsequently plucked up the courage and the matter was discussed openly. The outcome was that the couple agreed mutually to wait until better financial circumstances prevailed. The woman was perhaps unsure she had made the right decision as she loved her husband and did not want to offend his wishes but had asked the question to confirm her own beliefs. All this was revealed within the pattern of the tarot spread.

2

THE
ASTROLOGY SPREAD

The Astrology Spread is rightfully a popular one because
not only is each of the positions of the spread defined by
the astrological houses, or areas of life, but it also relates
to a particular astrological sign and season of the year
helping predictions to be dated.

The layout (page 120) is a simple one. After the cards
have been shuffled and returned to you, starting at the
nine o'clock position and in a clockwise direction, lay
twelve cards from the top of the pack to each of the
positions of the hands of a clock finishing at what would
be eight o'clock. Now offer the cards to the questioner
asking them to select one card which you then place into
the centre of the spread as its ruler. This card has the
special significance of indicating the overall positive or
negative outcome of the cards within the spread.

The spread is read in a clockwise direction for the past
and its circumstances and in an anticlockwise direction
for the future. Each card governs a period of one month
or one year so it is possible to make predictions over a
24-year period, that is twelve years back and twelve years
forward. However, this spread is best used for a one year
cycle with each card indicating one month in turn from
the time of the reading. The astrological houses and the
cards placed in them also give clues as to active areas of
the individual's life. The following list is given so that
you may best understand how to apply the energy of the
card in each house.

1st House	The self and present circumstances
2nd House	Financial situation
3rd House	Brothers, sisters and education
4th House	Home environment; the mother
5th House	Romance, luck and children to come
6th House	Work, health and income sources
7th House	Partnerships, business or marital
8th House	Death, inheritance and lawsuits
9th House	Overseas travel, higher education, aspirations
10th House	Career, promotional progress and ability; the father
11th House	Friends, neighbours and associates
12th House	Hidden matters, fears, self-undoing

Thus, with the knowledge of where to look for the answers to questions asked, the spread can be as simple or as complex as you require to make it. As in astrology, cards opposite act in opposition, adjacent cards act in conjunction and cards four places away from each other act as spurs or helpers, while those three places away indicate challenges. An appropriate astrology text will help to develop your skill in using this spread. It can be used to great effect with only the information provided here. You will find this spread one of the most informative and revealing of all.

Sample Readings using the Astrology Spread

A client asks if money will improve in the coming year. Check the 2nd, 6th and 10th houses as these relate to income, possessions and how the client will earn their money. Balance the effect of these three houses and weigh it against the 12th house for hidden bills or debts and perhaps lawsuits indicated in the 8th house.

A client asks if the partner they have will become a husband in the coming year. Check the 5th house of romance and the 7th house of partnerships and then the 11th house of friendships. If any cards present represent

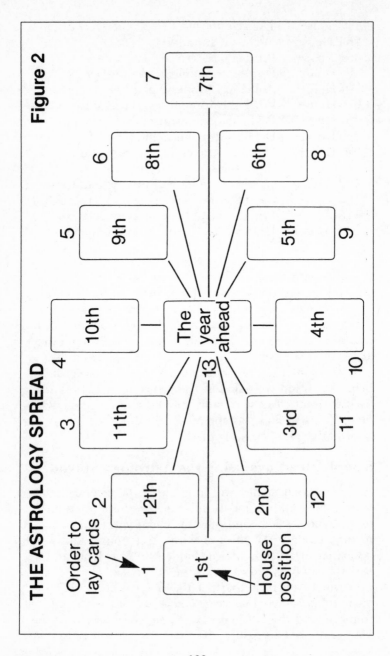

THE ASTROLOGY SPREAD

Figure 2

Order to lay cards

House position

gatherings and celebrations then the answer is positive.

Remember that the year begins from the month the reading commences with although the houses themselves relate to the signs of the zodiac in order, thus 1st house is Aries and rules that time of year, 2nd house Taurus and so on. Also note that the four suits of the tarot relate to the four elements of astrology and are well or badly placed as indicated in the chapters of the minor arcana giving another clue as to how their energies can manifest in everyday life. This spread may require more practice than most but is well worth the effort and patience required in its mastery to obtain clarity and accuracy of interpretation and prediction.

3
THE
SIX CARD SPREAD

The last of the spreads considered is another simple
question and answer device which you can use to confirm
prognostications from more complex readings. The cards
are shuffled in the normal manner and then held in the
left hand by the questioner and cut into three piles. The
three piles are then turned face up and the top card from
each pile placed below that pile as illustrated opposite.
The left-hand pile top card governs the past
circumstances of the question asked, while the card below
it clarifies how this leads to the present. The centre pile
top card indicates the present circumstances, while the
card below it indicates how they may best be served or
projected into the future. The right-hand pile top card
indicates the future, while the lower indicates how this
future will affect the questioner.

Sample Reading using the Six Card Spread

Question: Will my future at the company I work for
bring promotion and prosperity?
Card positions
The Past. Top, Eight of Pentacles. Bottom, Six of
Batons.
The past indicates hard work achieved and that
rewards were given for aims achieved. More effort had to
be ploughed back (Eight of Pentacles), in order that your
methods matched those of your employers (Six of
Batons).

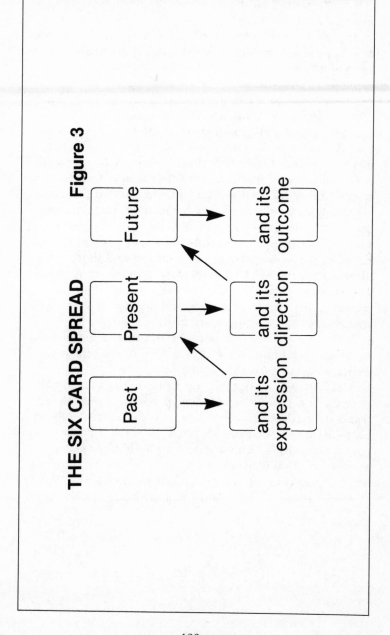

THE SIX CARD SPREAD

Figure 3

| Past | Present | Future |

and its expression

and its direction

and its outcome

The Present. Top, Page of Batons. Bottom, Queen of Swords.

The Page of Wands indicates that you are favoured or loved and liked by those who employ you while the Queen of Swords indicates that the way forward is through an older female who gained experience through her own errors and has the advice to secure your future. Her enmity could bring about your dismissal.

The Future. Top, Judgement. Bottom, The Emperor.

Judgement in the future position indicates that you will be measured on merit. Others will not be favoured over you through friendship or other means but failure in responsibility for your work will be accounted for. New beginnings can mean a job move in the future but the final card, the Emperor, indicates that positions of power, strength and trust can be won from your present position, if you are patient, do your job and don't undermine others. The Emperor here indicates that you gain more experience and thus will be given more responsibility. In this case I would advise the client to stay where they are and work at it.

I have for the past 15 years been a reader of the tarot cards and while my knowledge of it is competent now it grows with every reading and client I see.

The best way to become an expert is to practise and practise and then do some more practice. The athlete trains every day to hone his body to the shape to suit his particular event and even when at his or her peak continues to train. You are now an athlete of the tarot and must set your own training schedule. If you are not honest with yourself and your clients, you cheat only yourself and may never find the knowledge you sought at its beginning.

NOTES